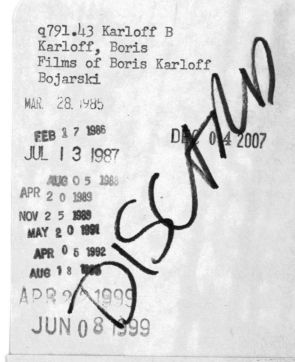

The FILMS of
BORIS KARLOFF

The FILMS of
BORIS KARLOFF

by RICHARD BOJARSKI
and Kenneth Beale

The Citadel Press · Secaucus, New Jersey

Acknowledgments

We want to thank the following for their special assistance and use of photographs: Embassy Pictures, William K. Everson, John Giriat, Luis Gasca, Culver Pictures, Zita Johann, Helen Killeen (UA Television), Marc Sonnenschein, Dick Smith, Sandrino Giglio (Casolaro Giglio Film Distributing Corp.), Stanley Simon, Paramount Pictures, Allied Artists, Steve Jochsberger, Bob Marcella (Official Films), Harry Nadler, Bob Burns, Cecil J. Miller, Charles Fellerman (AIP), Peter Bogdanovich, Ray Markham, Ken Vose, Loraine Burdick, Sheila Whitaker (British Film Institute), Jack Hardy, George E. Turner, Mrs. Richard Cotten, Mrs. Edgar Rowe, Susan Davis (University of Wisconsin), Gerald D. McDonald, Universal Pictures, John Cocchi, Crown-International, Cannon Releasing Corp., Mary Yushak (Museum of Modern Art), Gary Levinson, Art Ross, Marcela Palafox, 20th Century-Fox, Columbia Pictures, Ken Jones, Rembrandt Films, Al Soma, Mike McKay, Janus Barfoed (Danish Film Museum), Vitaprint, Don Fellman, Ray Gain, Armando Del Moral (Grafica Magazine), James J. Badal, Eric Hoffman, Bob Scherl, Max Stratyner, Harry Fiyalko, Ron Borst, Romano Tozzi, Bob Smith (Movie Poster Service), Steve and Erwin Vertlieb, Dion McGregor, Charles L. Turner, Metro-Goldwyn-Mayer, Bob Price, Joe Judice, Wes Shank, Richard Feiner & Company, Inc., George Stover, Alan Barbour, Richard Mirissis, Leonard Maltin, David Barnes, Saul Goodman, Joe Franklin, Fred von Bernewitz, Bernie Velleman, John Antosiewicz, Neil Sullivan of Mutual Films, Richard W. Bann, John McCabe, and Larry Byrd.

And special thanks to Bert Grey, whose contribution and inspiration led to the creation of this book.

First edition
Copyright ©1974 by Richard Bojarski and Kenneth Beale
All rights reserved
Published by Citadel Press
A division of Lyle Stuart, Inc.
120 Enterprise Ave., Secaucus, N. J. 07094
In Canada: George J. McLeod Limited
73 Bathurst St., Toronto 2B, Ont.
Manufactured in the United States of America by
Printed in the United States of America by
Noble Offset Printers, New York, N. Y.
Designed by William Meinhardt
Library of Congress catalog card number: 71-147832
ISBN 0-8065-0396-3

To
OUR WONDERFUL PARENTS

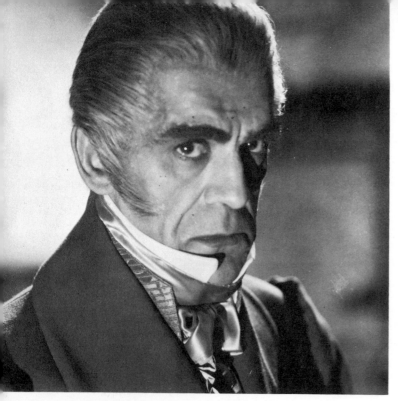
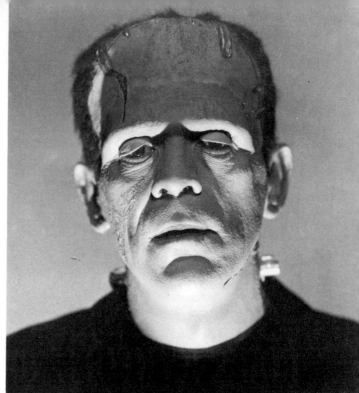

Contents

BORIS KARLOFF: Biography	11	The Black Cat	95
Early Films	36	The Gift of Gab	98
Silent Films	37	The Bride of Frankenstein	100
Sound Films	46	The Black Room	105
Graft	50	The Raven	109
Five Star Final	52	The Invisible Ray	112
The Mad Genius	54	The Walking Dead	116
The Yellow Ticket	56	The Man Who Lived Again	119
Guilty Generation	57	Juggernaut	121
Frankenstein	58	Charlie Chan at the Opera	123
Tonight or Never	64	Night Key	125
Behind the Mask	65	West of Shanghai	127
Business and Pleasure	67	The Invisible Menace	129
Scarface	68	Mr. Wong, Detective	131
The Cohens and Kellys in Hollywood	70	Son of Frankenstein	133
The Miracle Man	71	The Mystery of Mr. Wong	138
Night World	73	Mr. Wong in Chinatown	140
The Old Dark House	75	The Man They Could Not Hang	142
The Mask of Fu Manchu	79	Tower of London	145
The Mummy	83	The Fatal Hour	149
The Ghoul	87	British Intelligence	150
The Lost Patrol	90	Black Friday	152
The House of Rothschild	93	The Man with Nine Lives	156
		Devil's Island	159

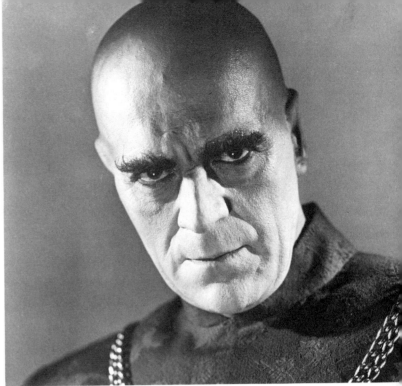

Doomed to Die	162
Before I Hang	164
The Ape	167
You'll Find Out	170
The Devil Commands	172
Information Please	175
The Boogie Man Will Get You	176
The Climax	178
House of Frankenstein	182
The Bodysnatcher	186
Isle of the Dead	190
Bedlam	194
The Secret Life of Walter Mitty	198
Lured	200
Unconquered	202
Dick Tracy Meets Gruesome	204
Tap Roots	207
Abbott and Costello	
Meet the Killer, Boris Karloff	210
The Strange Door	212
The Black Castle	215
Abbott and Costello	
Meet Dr. Jekyll and Mr. Hyde	218
Monster of the Island	222

The Hindu	224
Voodoo Island	226
The Haunted Strangler	228
Frankenstein 1970	230
Days of Thrills and Laughter	233
The Raven	235
Corridors of Blood	238
The Terror	240
Comedy of Terrors	243
Black Sabbath	245
Bikini Beach	248
Die, Monster, Die	249
Ghost in the Invisible Bikini	251
The Daydreamer	253
The Venetian Affair	254
The Sorcerers	256
Mad Monster Party	258
Targets	259
The Crimson Cult	262
The Snake People	265
The Incredible Invasion	267
Cauldron of Blood	269
BORIS KARLOFF on Television	273
Afterword	286

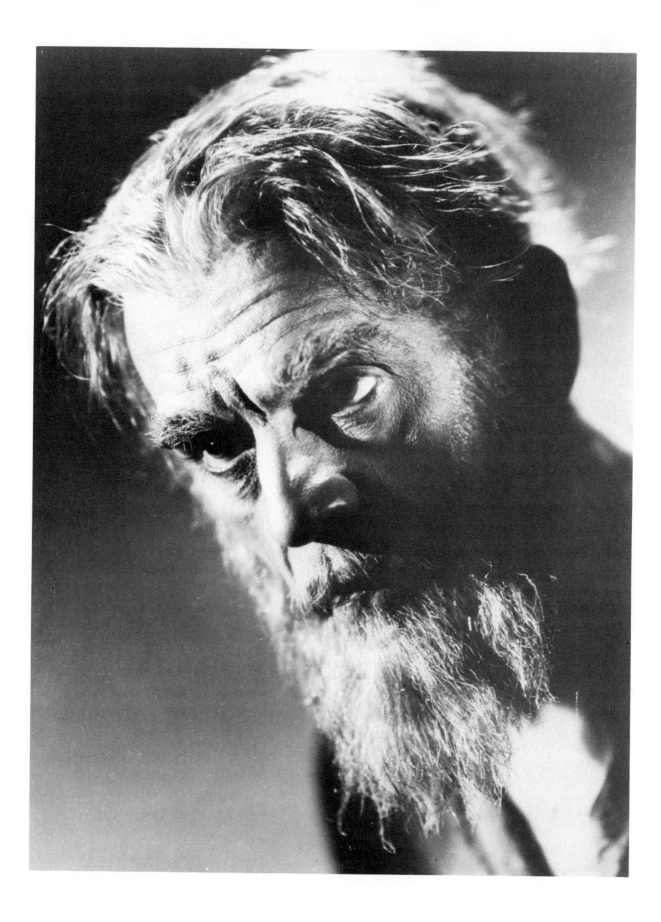

BORIS KARLOFF:
Biography

As a student in King's College in England.

Karloff at the age of three and a half.

BORIS KARLOFF: Biography

Boris Karloff, the English–born actor who brought life to Mary Shelley's words—and chilling death on the screen—appeared in over 150 films over a span of fifty years. The soft–spoken actor, whose lisping accent was a stock commodity in every impressionist's repertoire, was one of the few screen actors billed by his last name only. His performance as the Monster in *Frankenstein* and similar roles made his very name synonomous with "horror" (a term he disliked). Long before his death, he had achieved a mythological immortality in the dark waters of the imagination for generations to come.

Like his famous contemporaries, Bela Lugosi and Lon Chaney Jr., Karloff's off–screen self was the antithesis of his screen image. To his close circle of friends, he was a cultured, shy individual who shunned the limelight and enjoyed attending cricket and rugby matches. (During the thirties, he represented Hollywood in a cricket game against an Australian team headed by Bradman and McCabe, two of the greatest players.) Because of his personal, uphill struggle for recognition, he was constantly concerned for his fellow actors' welfare. In the thirties, he helped create the Screen Actors Guild.

11

As Father Whalen in a stock company production of *The Parish Priest* in 1914.

For Karloff, success did not come easily. He was over thirty when he appeared in his first film, *His Majesty, the American* (1919). This was followed by a succession of "bits" to supporting roles in sixty-odd films during a precarious twelve-year period before *Frankenstein* (1931). When he finally achieved star billing in *The Old Dark House* (1932), he was almost forty-five. The actor always acknowledged his gratitude to *Frankenstein* for the turning point in his career and never felt superior to that role. He later remarked, "The Monster was inarticulate, helpless and tragic, but I owe everything to him. He's my best friend." Appreciative of his hard-won fame, he accepted his monster image philosophically, rarely disappointing his public with a poor performance.

Though approximately fifty of his films are in the horror category, the remaining number usually found him cast either as a villainous Indian in *The Last of the Mohicans* (1920), a sadistic sailor in *Forbidden Cargo* (1925), a "North Woods" murderer in *Phantoms of the North* (1929) and even a "red herring" in *Lured* (1947). A few exceptions found him in "normal roles," but these were few and far between. Film producers, fearing disappointment from the public, again buried the actor in makeup, as his Chinese detective characterizations in the *Mr. Wong* series (1938–40) and his strangely unimpressive performance as a faithful Choctaw Indian servant in *Tap Roots* (1948). His few straight roles (unhampered by makeup or malevolence) were a nightclub owner in *Night World* (1932), an unjustly imprisoned French doctor in *Devil's Island* (1940) and a scientist caught in a web of intrigue in *The Venetian Affair* (1967). Though the horror-philes regard the richest period of his career from 1931 to 1946, one-third of his credits were "B" programmers, of which an occasional film descended into the "C" category, as in: *Voodoo Island* (1957). Aside from periodic ventures into theatre, radio and television, his screen career has been a prolific one. Not counting features, his lengthy credits also included narrations, voice-overs for animated cartoons and even five serials.

Christened William Henry Pratt, he was born in November 23, 1887 to a respectable, middle-

12

class family in the Camberwell suburb of London. He was the last child in a family of eight sons and a daughter. His father, Edward Pratt, was in the Indian consular service, as were his older brothers. Both his parents died during his childhood, and young William was raised by an "amiable sister and seven stern, older brothers." It was assumed that the youngest Pratt would follow in the footsteps of the others and enter the consular service. (One brother later became a judge in Bombay and another a governor of an Indian province.) But the one William admired the most was George, who experienced a brief career on the stage. In trying to emulate him, he obtained his first acting role at the age of ten in a Christmas church play, *Cinderella*. His role was a symbol of his future screen image to come, the "Demon King." Completing his schooling at Merchant Taylor's School and Uppingham, he was pressured by his older brothers to apply at King's College to study for the consular service. But the stage was his sole interest and he was not at any time desirous for the diplomatic career that his elder brothers planned for him. He later said, "Frankly, I was lazy, uninterested and did no work. I probably wouldn't have passed the exams anyway." Aware that he was at the crossroads of his life, he decided to leave home. "My first term reports revealed I attended more plays than classes," he said. "I was becoming a disgrace to the family name. In those days, black sheep in England either went to Canada or Australia." To decide his destination, he flipped a coin. Australia lost. After learning the Canadian provinces were encouraging immigration, he secured second–class passage and sailed from Liverpool to Ontario in May 1909.

Following some halfhearted attempts to learn farming, he decided to try acting. Learning there were opportunities in Vancouver, he used the remainder of his inheritance for train fare. Arriving with barely a pound to his name, he looked in vain for theatrical work. Broke, he took a pick–and–shovel job with the B. C. Electrical Company for $2.80 a day. After unsuccessful periods as a real estate salesman and a farmhand, he again approached several Vancouver stock companies, to no avail. Then his luck changed.

"I was feeling rather sorry for myself," he re-

In one of his early stock company roles.

called, "when I spotted an ad concerning a theatrical agent named Kelly in nearby Seattle in an old copy of *Billboard*. I immediately journeyed to Seattle and presented myself to him. After shamelessly telling him all the plays I'd acted in and that I was forced to sacrifice my career temporarily for my health, I informed him that I was now healthy and ready for a comeback." Two months later, while clearing land for a survey party, he heard from the agent. He was told to join the Ray Brandon Players, appearing in Kamloops, a mining town northeast of Vancouver. During the train trip there, he invented his stage name. "I dredged up 'Karloff' from Russian ancestors on my mother's side and I picked 'Boris' out of the chilly, Canadian air."

Totally unfamiliar with the rudiments of stage

Helene Vivian Soule, the actor's first wife.

directions and timing, he presented himself to the company manager hoping for the best. His first role was that of a sixty-year-old banker in Ferenc Molnar's *The Devil*. Then he unintentionally bumped into stage furniture, missed cues and literally pulverized the director's patience. He later recalled, "At the end of the performance, as I was slinking away to some dark corner, the manager came towards me with a malevolent gleam in his eye. 'Karloff, you know darn well you've never acted before. Still, we like you and you'll stay with us. . . .' " Though his salary was cut in half, he was an actor at last. He soon discovered he was popular in villainous roles. "I liked 'heavy' roles," he said, "and later in pictures I always sought them." After the troupe folded in Regina, Saskatchewan, a cyclone hit the town, leaving him stranded. When he emerged from the wreckage, he found all his belongings gone. Out of funds, he obtained a job aiding the natives in clearing away the debris. Shortly after, he succeeded in obtaining a position with the Harry St. Clair Players, another minor stock company. The group played small towns on both sides of the Canadian border. In some towns they played a week, in others they would be fortunate in settling down for a run. During a "run" in Minot, North Dakota, the company played fifty-three consecutive weeks where he played 106 parts. The actor was a quick study—and the quickest study got the longest parts. "Having a peculiar faculty for learning lines easily, I always drew the biggest part. Half the time, the director simply picked out the part with the most pages and tossed it to me," he recalled. The actor learned his craft by playing leads in such traditional pieces as *Way Down East, Charley's Aunt, East Lynne, Paid in Full,* etc. Standards were low. *The Fortune Hunter,* which called for a cast of twenty, was put on with only eight people—one of them a local housewife. Frequently they would eliminate the third act, if they felt tired. "We all took turns minding the box office and being stage manager. And in those days we never had a prop or even a dress rehearsal," said Karloff. "Although our audiences were usually made up of farm workers and lumberjacks, their taste in dramas was impeccable."

During this period the young actor managed to live with very little money. He bought his

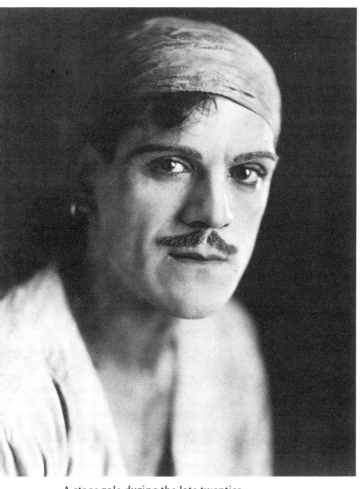

A stage role during the late twenties.

and left with Billie Bennett's road company of *The Virginian*. The group played the West for a year, and ended in Los Angeles in late 1917. The actor secured engagements with a few stock companies traveling up and down the California coast. But this was interrupted by the influenza epidemic of 1918, which caused many theatres to shut down. To make ends meet, he reverted back to day-laboring — loading and unloading heavy sacks of flour from trucks. After two months of this, he returned to Los Angeles hoping to get some vaudeville work. When this fell through, he finally turned to the film studios. Through an agent, he picked up a few days' work as a $5-a-day extra in Douglas Fairbanks' *His Majesty, the American*. Hoping for further film work, he continued to haunt the studios. With the aid of a sympathetic female agent, he obtained other minor roles.

The following year (1920) saw him in his first important role, as a murderous French-Canadian trapper in *The Deadlier Sex*. The part, and his Canadian background, typed him in such roles for a while. During the silent period, long before

clothes in local pawnshops and lived in "no-cooking" boarding houses where he learned to fry an egg on the bottom of an inverted flatiron. "Sometimes I barely managed to stay alive," he said.

After two years with the St. Clair Players, he decided to try his luck in the larger theatrical centers and headed for Chicago. But the Windy City was in the midst of a theatrical slump. World War I had meanwhile broken out, and he attempted to enlist in the British army, but was rejected due to a heart murmur. Returning to St. Clair, he stayed on for another year, continuing to play the Western provinces of Canada and the Northwestern United States. But he realized his chance for any theatrical success lay in the big cities. Trying Chicago again, he had better luck

Being escorted by makeup man Jack Pierce to the *Frankenstein* set.

With Bela Lugosi in 1932.

"speech" was important, Karloff's British accent was considered a "put-on" rather than an asset by assistant directors. They scornfully imitated his cultured accent and polite manners. "Why don't you try climbing down that high horse?" they would sarcastically remark. "You know you ain't foolin' nobody by that stuff." In 1923, however, Hollywood went into a production slump. He discovered he couldn't return to stock since movies were rapidly making the stock companies obsolete. Aware that registering with the Central Casting Bureau for extra work would end his hopes for going any higher, he was forced to take a day-laboring job. He drove a truck for a building materials company for six months while continuing to seek roles at the studios. That same year, he married Helene Vivian Soule, a dancer. The marriage terminated in divorce in 1928.

During the 1920s, his dark, brooding looks got him villainous roles of various sizes for inde-pendent companies like Vitagraph, Sunset and Gotham. In *Dynamite Dan* (1924), he was a scheming "heavy"; in *Parisian Nights* (1925), he was a sadistic French apache; and in *Forbidden Cargo* (1925), he played a cruel mate on a rum-running ship, who tried to pour molten lead into the eyes of the hero. Though most of his appearances in these minor melodramas went unnoticed, he played a role, regardless of its size, for all it was worth. In a Pauline Frederick tear-jerker of the mid-twenties (*Her Honor, the Governor*), a critic commented briefly on his performance: ". . . Snipe Collins, a weak creature half-crazed with drugs, is well played by Boris Karloff. Many such a wretch has been dragged into Police Headquarters. His shaken, jerky figure, the twitching mouth, the vicious anger which vents itself on a helpless man who has tormented him for years, is, next to Miss Frederick's, the most authentic piece of work in the picture. . . ."

16

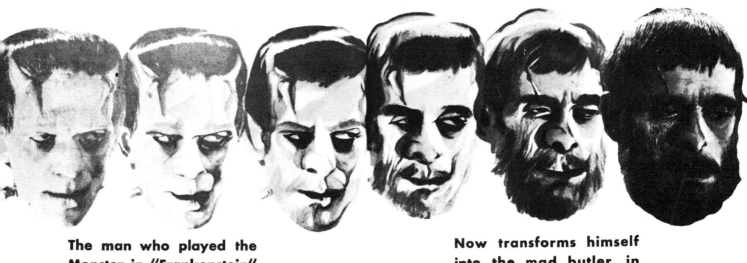

The man who played the
Monster in "Frankenstein"

Now transforms himself
into the mad butler, in

"THE OLD DARK HOUSE"

A characterization that will
make the world talk!

Screen acting that lifts the
screen to new heights!

Another whale of a pic-
ture directed by James
Whale, who also directed
"Frankenstein"

Produced by
Carl Laemmle, Jr.

Presented by
Carl Laemmle

with
KARLOFF
MELVYN
DOUGLAS

And CHARLES LAUGHTON, who
stole "The Devil and The Deep!"

And GLORIA STUART, who steals
your heart and soul!

The best-selling novel by J. B. Priestley
comes to life and chizzles your backbone!

STEP OUT
WITH
UNIVERSAL

STEP OUT
WITH
UNIVERSAL

The picture that should have made his reputation—but didn't—came in 1926. He was given
the major part of a sinister mesmerist in the film
version of *The Bells,* an old Henry Irving stage
success. Opposite Lionel Barrymore, he gave an
effective performance, using many of the stares
and mannerisms that later became familiar to
moviegoers. But producers failed to cast him into
similar roles, and he returned to undistinguished
minor roles like a native chief in *Tarzan and the
Golden Lion* (1927). During this discouraging
period in Hollywood, he met Lon Chaney, the
master of makeup (whose macabre reputation he
was later to inherit). Chaney encouraged him,
telling him that the secret of success in pictures
lay in being different.

To gain attention from movie producers, he

began to alternate his film work with stage appearances in Los Angeles and San Francisco. He
appeared in *Window Panes, Kongo, Hotel Im-
perial* and *The Idiot,* drawing minor critical
notices.

Sound arrived, and in 1929 he made his talkie
debut in *Behind That Curtain.* He had a small
role in this early *Charlie Chan* talkie. But he
fared better in his next film, *The Unholy Night,*
directed by his old colleague, Lionel Barrymore.
Impressed by Karloff's ability, Barrymore enlarged his small part of a mysterious Hindu. Although his stage background helped him survive
the transition from silents, he continued to obtain
the usual run of minor "heavy" roles. In these, he
usually received a thrashing at the hands of the
hero, winding up as a corpse, or worse. At forty-

17

two, he later said, "I had stopped writing home, because I had nothing to write about." But in 1930 the tide finally turned. Between films, he wandered into the Actor's Equity office to pick up his mail. A tip from the receptionist promptly sent him to the Belasco Theatre, where *The Criminal Code,* a New York stage success was being cast. Karloff immediately arrived at the theatre and obtained a role in the Martin Flavin play. Though it was a minor part, it was an important one: Galloway, the prison trusty who becomes a killer. The show ran for nine weeks in San Francisco and Los Angeles. On the strength of his performance, he married for the second time, to Dorothy Stine, a Michigan girl working as a children's librarian in Los Angeles. Soon Columbia Pictures bought the film rights and signed him to repeat his stage role. "That was the first real break I ever had," he said. "One of the larger studios with a bigger list of contract players, might have bought *The Criminal Code* and I might have been out of luck. At last I realized I hadn't struggled in vain." His busiest screen period followed. During 1931–32, twenty-three of his films were released: an average of nearly one a month. Though his roles didn't increase in size, the vehicles increased in importance. He played opposite Richard Dix in *Young Donovan's Kid* and *The Public Defender,* and with Edward G. Robinson in *Smart Money* and *Five Star Final.*

He worked with Lionel Barrymore again in *The Yellow Ticket,* and with his brother John Barrymore in *The Mad Genius.*

Then in mid–1931, Universal cast him as a gangster in a newspaper melodrama, *Graft.* The studio was impressed enough with the result to test him for the role of the Monster for their upcoming production, *Frankenstein.* He described it thus: "While I was eating lunch at the Universal Studio commissary, someone tapped me on the shoulder and said that Mr. Whale would like to see me at his table. Jimmy Whale was then the hottest director on the lot and told me he was getting ready to shoot the Mary Shelley classic, *Frankenstein,* and would like to test me for the Monster." Many actors had been tested for the role. Originally Universal assigned Robert Florey as director. Bela Lugosi, who had just completed *Dracula,* was to star. At any rate, both star and director were replaced. Whale was given the picture instead, while Florey and Lugosi did *Murders in the Rue Morgue.*

Whale said: "Karloff's face fascinated me. I made drawings of his head, added sharp bony ridges where I imagined the skull might have joined. His physique was weaker than I could wish, but that queer, penetrating personality of his, I felt, was more important than his shape, which could easily be altered." Jack Pierce, Universal's head makeup man, was assigned to create

With Jack Pierce in the Universal Pictures makeup department.

A family reunion with his brothers while making *The Ghoul* in England.

the final makeup design. Pierce spent late hours experimenting with the actor after weeks of research. Frankenstein's staggering, scarred, flat-headed creation with heavy-lidded lizard eyes and bolted neck slowly emerged. Whale made the test, liked it, and showed it to Carl Laemmle, in charge of production. Laemmle approved. He liked Karloff's eyes. "They mirrored the sufferings of the poor dumb creature, in contrast to his frightful appearance and hideous strength."

From Karloff: "A fascinating job—he had no speech and hardly any intelligence, yet you had to convey a tragic part. Half a dozen actors tested for the part but I was the lucky one. I say 'lucky' because any one of them probably would have played it just as well as I did—and would also have reaped the benefits that came to me. But despite the fact that the picture made me . . . it was a rather horrible experience . . . the makeup was quite an ordeal. I had to arrive at the studio every morning at 5:30 and spend three and a half hours in the makeup chair getting ready for

Celebrating Carl Laemmle's 67th birthday with James Scott, Hugh Enfield, Ken Maynard, Carl Laemmle, Vince Barnett, Margaret Sullavan, Andy Devine and Carl Laemmle Jr.

19

A studio artist's conception of Karloff as *Bluebeard,* a film Universal never made.

the day's work . . . the makeup itself was quite painful, particularly the putty used on my eyes. There were many days when I thought I would never be able to hold out until the end of the day, but somehow or other I always did."

To increase his size for the role, he wore a doubly quilted suit beneath. Unfortunately, *Frankenstein* was shot in midsummer, and he was left sopping wet. To avoid being uncomfortable, he changed his underclothing at intervals, but often felt damp from his previous undergarments. He later said, "Throughout the filming, I felt as if I were wearing a shroud, which no doubt added to the realism." During the laboratory scenes where the Monster was created amid booming thunder and flashes of lightning, the actor said: "I was never as nervous during the entire filming as when I lay half-naked and strapped to the operating table. Above me I could see the special effects men shaking the white-hot scissorlike car-

bons that simulated the lightning. I prayed very hard that no one got butterfingers."

Though a great deal of the success of *Frankenstein* resulted from James Whale's skillful direction, Karloff never hesitated to praise Jack Pierce's makeup, "When you get right down to it, it was Jack Pierce who really created the Frankenstein Monster. I was merely the animation in the costume."

When the film finally premiered in Santa Barbara, he was so initially subordinate to the stars of the film, Colin Clive and Mae Clarke, he was not invited to attend. It was only after the film's release that the Universal executives realized who the public was truly interested in: not the romantic leads (today only a couple of footnotes in cinema history), but the Monster. They hastened to put him under contract. When his agent called him with the news, the actor sighed happily with relief, "After twenty years of acting, for once I'll

Karloff in 1936.

know where my next breakfast is coming from!" The film grossed twelve million dollars from its original $250,000 investment and helped snowball the horror cycle even more than its predecessor, *Dracula*. All manner of films were planned for him by the studio, including a remake of *The Hunchback of Notre Dame* and *The Invisible Man*. But the Monster dogged Karloff until the actor's death. Not only did fans send him voodoo dolls, but he was also the butt of much Hollywood gallows humor. For years, Groucho Marx's standard greeting was, "How much do you charge to haunt a house?"

To build up their new star, Universal's publicity department decided to emphasize mystery. They barred visitors to his set, forbade interview-

Raising baby turkeys on his Beverly Hills property.

ers to see him without makeup, and eliminated the usual personal appearances. At the beginning, he privately harbored reservations about his studio's approach and resented being imprisoned by his screen image. Universal soon modified its attempts to make him into a "successor" to Lon Chaney after they discovered the public's acceptance of him as more than a mere curiosity. "After my next few films showed satisfactory returns," he said, "the studio ended the nonsense of not appearing in public without my makeup on."

Universal, aware of the public's appetite for more horror films, lost no time in shaping new grotesqueries around their new star. Hoping to duplicate the success of *Frankenstein,* they reunited him and its director in *The Old Dark House,* adapted from J. B. Priestley's novel. Departing from stereotyped melodrama like *The Bat* and *The Cat and the Canary,* Whale avoided the usual clutching hands, hooded figures and secret panels and instead relied on a skillful mixture of characterization, macabre humor and atmosphere. Karloff's appearance was altered again by Jack Pierce for his role as the homicidal butler, Morgan. This film marked his first starring role. Critics and public both liked it, and demanded more. The studio then loaned him out to MGM, which cast him as the evil Chinese genius in *The Mask of Fu Manchu.* Since his previous horror roles contained no dialogue, the public flocked to the theatres to hear him speak. Although he later played other Oriental roles, this was his most successful. In spite of later inter-

pretations of the Sax Rohmer character, Karloff's performance was rated the best of them all.

Again, the comparison to Lon Chaney was brought up. Karloff disclaimed any resemblance. "Chaney had his own distinct way of playing a bizarre character with whom the audience sympathized. My type is one in which sympathy is diverted to the romantic leads of the picture. I could never follow Chaney's footsteps and would not want to. We each had our own styles of work."

But it was not until his appearance in *The Mummy,* that his reputation was firmly established. Karl Freund, who had photographed many fine German silents, was chosen to direct. The actor's makeup in this film was the most uncomfortable he ever wore during his entire screen career. Aside from his torso and limbs, which were covered with rotting bandages, Jack Pierce covered his entire features with cotton, rubber cement and paint, transforming him into a centuries–old Egyptian. Like *Frankenstein* and *Dracula,* this film set the pattern for a long series of sequels and imitations. In spite of his films accumulating large profits for his studio, the actor's salary still remained below $400 a week. Among the film projects Universal had lined up for him were *Bluebeard, The Wizard* (scripted by John Huston) and *Destination Unknown.* Only the last film was made, with Ralph Bellamy replacing Karloff.

At this time, Karloff and his wife lived in a small home beside Toluca Lake. He had a garden, an extensive library, and three Scottish ter-

At home with his second wife (Dorothy Stine) in 1937.

riers. As a star, he did not conform to the usual pattern of extravagance. He drove a small Ford coupe, and avoided the movie colony's lavish social affairs. Asked if he'd ever gone to one, he replied, "Yes, just one. We felt that we had to go for business reasons, and for two hours Mrs. Karloff and I were in abject misery. Such things are all right for those who enjoy them, but I guess we're not built that way." He was a charter member of the Hollywood Cricket Club. Prominent among its members were British fellow actors Ronald Colman and C. Aubrey Smith.

Unable to get a salary increase, he left Universal in early 1933 and accepted an offer from Gaumont–British to make *The Ghoul.* He returned to his native England for the first time in twenty–four years and was reunited with three of his brothers: Sir John Pratt, in charge of Chinese affairs at the London Foreign Office; Mr. Justice Charles M. Pratt, former judge of the High Court of Bombay, India; and F. G. Pratt, C. S. I., former governor of an Indian province. The film, however, turned out to be a disappointment. The critics and the public claimed that the tale of an Egyptologist returning from the dead to reclaim a stolen gem, was an obvious reworking of *The Mummy.*

Returning to Hollywood, he free–lanced and obtained two "straight" roles in two major films. In the elaborate George Arliss vehicle, *The House of Rothschild,* he convincingly portrayed the scheming Baron Ledrantz. In John Ford's *The Lost Patrol,* he gave a memorable performance as the pathetic soldier, Sanders. Impressed by these favorable notices, Universal drew up another contract, giving him a raise in salary. He also obtained the right to free–lance at other studios throughout the length of his contract.

Universal originally wanted to star him in *A Trip to Mars* (based on a script by R. C. Sherriff), but decided to team him with their other horror star Bela Lugosi in *The Black Cat.* Supposedly based on Poe's poem, the far–fetched story–line of devil worship and revenge wisely gave equal prominence to both actors. Encouraged by solid box–office returns, the studio shrewdly combined the team with Poe again in *The Raven* the following year. In all, they made eight films together. Only in the first two, how-

The doting father with his two-month-old daughter, Sara Jane.

ever, did they receive equal treatment. Thereafter, one or the other dominated—usually Karloff, who said: "Poor old Bela, it was a strange thing. He was really a shy, sensitive, talented man who had a fine career on the classical stage in Europe. But he made a fatal mistake. He never took the trouble to learn our language. . . . He had real problems with his speech, and difficulty interpreting lines."

In 1935, Karloff returned to the role that his fans eagerly awaited. Again he subjected himself to Jack Pierce's makeup for his second screen appearance as the Monster in *The Bride of Frankenstein.* Whale again directed, and the film outdid the original in settings, photography and performances. Unlike *Frankenstein* it also had a stirring musical score by Franz Waxman. The script injected more scenes from Shelley's novel, making the Monster more sympathetic. It also made him articulate. (Karloff considered the last a mistake and tried to persuade Whale against this.) Many fans considered the film to be the best of the *Frankenstein* series and the peak of his cinematic career. Throughout the remainder of his life, he would never fail to be moved by letters from children expressing compassion for the Monster. "The kiddies really sympathized with the Monster. They . . . knew it wasn't the Monster's fault that he was so terrible. He just couldn't help it. So you see, they weren't actually frightened. I don't think anyone is, really—at least, not for more than a minute or two at a time."

By 1936 horror films had settled down into a predictable, programmer niche. Made on more modest budgets, they retained most of their popularity, but broke no more box-office records. Karloff still dominated them, with Lugosi ranking second. The duo co-starred in *The Invisible Ray,* playing scientists: Bela was sane, but Boris was a homicidal maniac. Thus he embarked upon the next phase of his unusual career. He was to repeat this part many times, throughout his life. Gradually he came to be identified as the perfect mad scientist. He played two similar roles in England, in *The Man Who Lived Again* and *Juggernaut.* Unexpectedly, production of chillers ground to a halt due to waning audience interest. Returning to Hollywood, he was given another chance at straight roles. However, routine melodramas like *West of Shanghai* and *The Invisible Menace* did little to utilize his abilities. Two exceptions were his interesting performances as an aging inventor in *Night Key* and the genial Chinese detective, Mr. Wong, in a series of Monogram programmers. More in his customary style were a group of radio programs he did in 1938: six dramatic appearances on the chilling "Lights Out" series (scripted by Arch Oboler).

During this period he responded to a question about his acting technique: "I am always myself until the moment I actually face the camera. I do not believe it is necessary for an actor to pace up and down the set, sometimes hours before he is ready to take a scene, screwing up his face, gesticulating and physically rehearsing over and over again. Personally, I have found the best results by memorizing my lines and actions mentally and producing the physical reaction when I am at work.

With Arch Oboler on the "Lights Out" radio show.

"It isn't that I have any particular aversion to rehearsing; on the contrary, I study and memorize every line I have to speak and every gesture I have to create, but I do it with a minimum of physical effort. I find myself better able to grasp a situation and character by the sole method of concentration."

Following the successful reissues of *Frankenstein* and *Dracula,* Universal executives discovered that horror films could still be profitably produced for domestic consumption. In late 1938, the studio signed Karloff to star in *Son of Frankenstein,* for his third appearance as the Monster. During the filming, his only child, Sara Jane, was born. The production, directed by Rowland V. Lee, was an ambitious attempt at recapturing the excitement of the previous films. It had a big budget, elaborate sets, and a fine cast, including Lugosi and Basil Rathbone. Though critics stated it did not equal *Bride* in quality, its success launched a second horror cycle. Karloff decided that he would never play Frankenstein's creation again, and he never did.* When the series went on with other actors, Karloff continued to get fan mail on his "appearances" in them. (Technically he did appear in the 1944 *House of Frankenstein,* but as a mad scientist.) Nevertheless, he had nothing but respect for his successors in the Monster's shoes. "Anybody who can take that makeup every morning deserves respect," he said.

Later that year (1939), Universal reunited him with Rathbone in *Tower of London,* a fine historical melodrama. Karloff's character was actually based on the story of the man who killed the two little princes in the Tower. The revival of screen terror encouraged the actor to resume his mad scientist role. He suspended life in ice, developed a life–giving serum and transplanted brains, hearts and other organs in a string of medical fantasies like *The Man They Could Not Hang, Black Friday, The Man With Nine Lives* and others.

In late 1940, this phase of his career came to an abrupt end. For the first time in a decade, he returned to the stage in Joseph Kesselring's play, *Arsenic and Old Lace.* It was Karloff's first time on Broadway and he was hesitant in accepting the offers of producers Lindsay and Crouse. "I was their first and only choice for the homicidal brother, Jonathan Brewster," he said, "but I held off when they asked me to come East for the role. I told them frankly that I'd play stock . . . in the sticks, but in the eyes of New York's playgoers I was strictly a film player and I'd be darned if I'd take a chance by starring in my first big–city play. If, I said, there were a couple of other parts better than mine it would be okay with me. As it turned out, of course, the two old aunts were the stars of the show, its very backbone, and what a splendid job they did! My part was simply mustard on a plate of good roast beef."

What decided him to accept was a line of dialogue. His character, asked why he'd killed someone, replies, "He said I looked like Boris Karloff." With a very nervous Karloff in the role of Jonathan, the show opened at the Fulton Theatre on January 10, 1941. It received excellent re-

* Not to be counted is a television appearance as the Monster on *Route 66,* many years later.

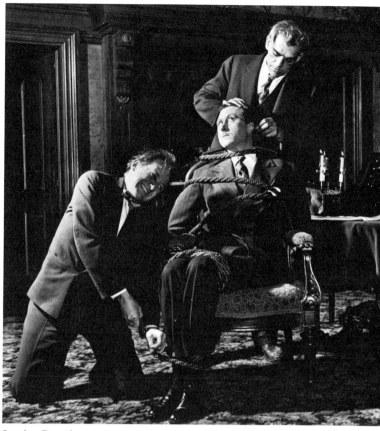

In the Broadway stage production of *Arsenic and Old Lace* with Edgar Stehli and Allyn Joslyn.

views, eventually running for more than 1400 performances. *The New York Times'* Brooks Atkinson said: "As the evil one, Mr. Karloff moves quietly through the plot and poison without resorting to trickeries"; from Richard Lockridge in the *Sun* came the comment: "he manages to be horrifying without really scaring the audience out of its laughter"; the *Post's* John Mason Brown called him "a bogeyman who could make goose-flesh, at any rate, out of a sow's ear." His fears proven groundless, he found that he enjoyed live theatre again. "Playing for an audience is a great joy after years of acting for the camera. . . . The most beautiful thing of all is the complete stillness of an audience so intent that it scarcely breathes. I had almost forgotten these things. In pictures the director is your only audience."

He continued in the play for three years, taking time out only to make a film he owed Columbia under an old contract. The film, *The Boogie Man Will Get You,* was a weak comedy spoof of his current stage success. He played the murder-

25

On the Universal lot in 1944 with Lon Chaney Jr. and former silent star, William Desmond.

ous Jonathan on the road, for servicemen, and (in later years) twice on television. Due to his stage commitment, Warner Bros. bypassed him in favor of Raymond Massey for the film version. Besides elevating him to the status of a Broadway star, the play also proved a financial windfall. The producers had persuaded him into investing $6,000 into it. The money was returned many times over.

During his stage run in New York, a different side of his personality was revealed to the public when he appeared on radio's "Information Please." The actor displayed mental agility opposite the show's panel: John Kiernan, Franklin P. Adams and Oscar Levant. A critic recalled, "Karloff was very modest. One of the few times he fumbled a guest's question was when it referred to the name of Dr. Frankenstein's assistant. But his batting average was good and the competition were anything but dopes."

Eventually, the actor's contract with *Arsenic and Old Lace* ended. "I wept the night I had to quit," he said, "and this in spite of a road tour of sixty–six weeks totalling over 1600 performances." But now he was able to sign a contract for a two–picture deal at Universal, at three times his former salary. The first of these, *The Climax,* was a

Attending a Screen Actors Guild meeting with Jane Wyman, Henry Fonda and Ronald Reagan.

26

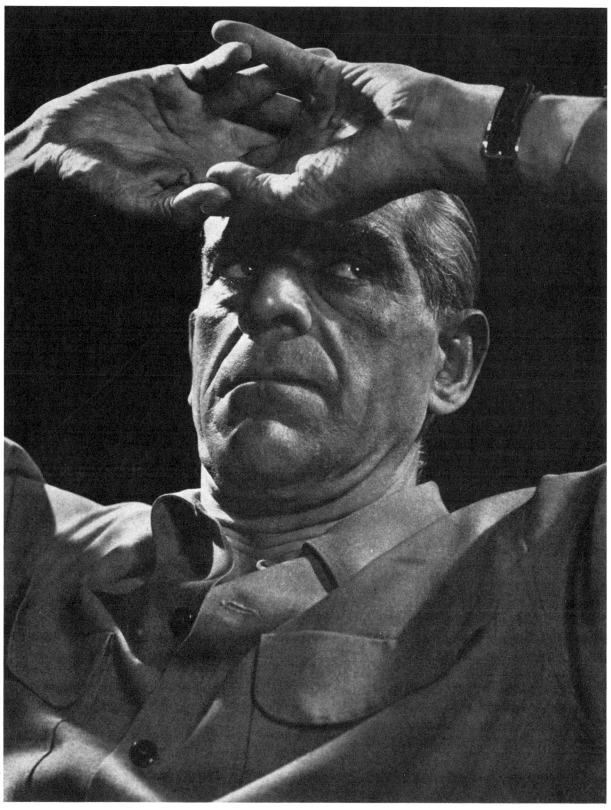

Karloff in 1948.

Helping to publicize the film *Abbott and Costello Meet Frankenstein* in New York City

remake of an early Jean Hersholt talkie. It was Karloff's first color film. Critics commented on its similarity in plot to *Phantom of the Opera,* which the studio successfully remade a year earlier. Fans grumbled a bit when Susanna Foster's singing interrupted his menace from time to time, but it was elaborate entertainment, appropriate for his return to the screen. He fared better in his next film, *House of Frankenstein.* The studio teamed him with their stable of monsters, the Wolf Man, Dracula and the Frankenstein Monster, now played by Glenn Strange. Karloff was in top form as Dr. Niemann, who restores them to life. Like their previous entries in the *Frankenstein* series, Universal's special effects, photography and production values made this a first–class chiller. In spite of World War II, or because of it, horror films were as popular as ever. But during this period, he did not dominate the scene as he had in the '30s. Part of the reason was the emergence of Lon Chaney Jr. as the new horror star at Universal. The versatile younger actor had effectively played nearly every one of the studio's horror creations, including the Frankenstein Monster; the other factor was the postwar decline in this category of screen entertainment. The second horror cycle petered out in the late '40s.

Although Universal led the other studios in the manufacture of chillers, Val Lewton's low–budget unit at RKO was producing a series of psychological horror films. Most of his films were finan-cial and critical hits, despite cast and story weaknesses. *The Bodysnatcher,* the first of three Lewton films to star Karloff, brought the star the most critical acclaim. His performance as the murderous coachman was unforgettable. It was the last classic horror role he was ever to make. The film was the last time he appeared with Lugosi, who had a conspicuously smaller role.

Karloff also appeared in *Isle of the Dead* and *Bedlam.* He said: "This series that I have been doing has measured up to what I consider a worthwhile artistic standpoint. Three men, Mark Robson, Robert Wise (directors) and Val Lewton have proved to be the very best working combination in my life. They're cultured and articulate, we thresh things out, go into reason . . . and I think the ultimate results bear every trace of it. I can't begin to tell you how happy this setup makes me." Plans to unite him with Lugosi in another film fell through when the new RKO heads canceled the producer's contract. Five years would pass before Karloff returned to the genre.

In 1946 the actor was divorced from his second wife, Dorothy. He then married for the third and final time, to the former Evelyn Hope Helmore, previously a story assistant to David O. Selznick.

With horror films in the doldrums, he obtained an opportunity to explore comedy and straight roles for a change. But most of these were a villainous nature. He turned up as an unexpected

Attending the *Samson and Delilah* premiere with his third wife (Evelyn Hope Helmore).

red herring in an excellent suspenser, *Lured;* in *The Secret Life of Walter Mitty,* he revealed a hidden ability for self–parody; in DeMille's *Unconquered,* he portrayed a rascally Seneca Indian chief outwitted by Gary Cooper; and in *Dick Tracy Meets Gruesome,* he was a criminal who was eventually captured by the famed comic–strip hero. But in *Tap Roots,* he portrayed his first sympathetic role in years, as another Indian. "As a matter of fact," he said, "Tishomingo is one of the few characters I've ever played on the screen who didn't come to a bad end." Paramount intended to cast him as the wicked King of the Philistines in DeMille's *Samson and Delilah,* but George Sanders replaced him.

In 1949, he made his debut in the new medium of television. From then on, he dedicated more and more of his time to it, doing little else between 1958 and 1963.

Following two Broadway flops (*The Linden Tree* and *The Shop at Sly Corner*), he attained success in the 1950 revival of J. M. Barrie's *Peter Pan,* opposite Jean Arthur. Leonard Bernstein contributed the music and lyrics, and Karloff thus made his singing bow. He had a good baritone voice, as the recordings of the show reveal. Wendy

With Ethel Griffies in the 1949 Broadway stage production of *The Shop at Sly Corner.*

29

As Captain Hook in the 1950 Broadway stage success, *Peter Pan*.

Toye (later a film director) co–directed, and the cast included Joe E. Marks and Nehemiah Persoff. Brooks Atkinson, the *Times* critic said:

This is Mr. Karloff's day of triumph. As the father of the Darling children and the pirate King, he is at the top of his bent. Although he is best known for the monsters he has played on stage and screen, Mr. Karloff is an actor of tenderness and humor, with an instinct for the exact inflection. His Captain Hook is a horrible cutthroat of the sea; and Mr. Karloff does not shirk the villainies. But they are founded on an excellent actor's enjoyment of an excellent part, and a relish of Barrie's inscrutable humors. There is something of the grand manner in the latitude of his style and the roll of his declamation; and there is withal an abundance of warmth and gentleness in his attitude toward the audience.

Of this role, Karloff said:

It would be easy to play Captain Hook so that I scared the pants off the children, but this would not be any fun for the audience or the play itself. I prefer to play Hook so the children can see the connection between the pirate and the father. . . . The best cue to the interpretation of Captain Hook may be found in James M. Barrie's own stage directions... Barrie describes Hook as "a public school man gone wrong," a rather direct poke at some of the pompous English gentlemen of his day.

30

Autographing photos of himself in New York City during a promotional tour of his film, *The Strange Door.*

After matinees, Karloff would invite children into his dressing room, and permit them to try on his hook. "The children in the audience, they are the stars now of *Peter Pan,"* he said. "They devour the parts, they act them out *for* you, they keep one step ahead of you all the time." Illustrating his fondness for children, he also narrated fairy tales and bedtime stories on the weekly half-hour radio program, "A Program for Children of All Ages."

In 1952, he and his wife moved from their New York apartment to London, to begin a new television series, "Colonel March of Scotland Yard." Its detective character gave him an opportunity to escape type-casting, but the series' low budget and routine format prevented it from becoming an international success. While there, he also accepted an offer to appear in *Monster of the Island,* a rarely seen Italian film. He continued to commute between the United States and England for film and television assignments, eventually moving to London for good in 1959.

He returned to Broadway for the last time in 1955, to portray the sympathetic Bishop Cauchon in Jean Anouilh's *The Lark,* which starred Julie Harris. In this Lillian Hellman adaptation were Christopher Plummer, Joseph Wiseman, and Theodore Bikel. A critical and commercial success, the play was recreated for television two years later, with Karloff repeating his role. Because the part was a complete departure from his villainous roles, he always referred to the play as the highest point of his career.

He said:

Though I am still pulling bits of the Monster's claws out of my back, I am literally still carrying the scars. Professionally, and you may not realize it, "Cauchon" here in *The Lark* is the first solid, successful, serious acting part I've had on Broadway. . . . And what a distinguished company. All of them, especially Julie Harris. She plays Joan with the hand of God.

31

Walter Kerr in the *Herald Tribune* said that he was "an agonized figure of great power and genuine warmth; the crumpled and baffled simplicity of his 'My pride is less than yours' is very touching"; and in *The Times,* Brooks Atkinson said, "Although Boris Karloff has been for years associated with hokum parts in the theatre, he is the paternal, sorrowful, pleading Cauchon . . . and he is admirable."

Hollywood had embarked on a science-fiction cycle in 1950, and the studios concentrated on the world being invaded by outer-space aliens. The scientists were now combating evil from without—not contributing to it. In the meantime, the horror film languished, falling behind the quality of the previous decade. Universal tried to revive the gothic horror film by casting Karloff in two interesting vehicles, *The Strange Door* and *The Black Castle.* He then appeared in a routine horror spoof, *Abbott and Costello Meet Dr. Jekyll*

Greeting an unidentified actor on the set of *Abbott and Costello Meet Dr. Jekyll and Mr. Hyde.*

and Mr. Hyde, opposite the two comics. But his next horror film was disappointing. He played a skeptical scientist in the dismal *Voodoo Island.* It became apparent that his name and presence were being used to raise the film from the level of the third-rate. He then went to England for *The Haunted Strangler* and *Corridors of Blood* (the U.S. release of the latter film was delayed for several years). Though Karloff was by now showing his age, he was still capable of an effective performance as a Jekyll-Hyde character in the *Strangler.*

It was not until 1957, however, that the third horror cycle really began. This was inspired by the television release of the old Universal horror films. The renaissance was further aided by the successful color remakes of *Frankenstein* and *Dracula* by England's Hammer Films. Finding himself in demand again for the old, familiar parts, Karloff accepted the starring role in *Frankenstein 1970.* He played the descendant of the original doctor in this unimaginative extension of the *Frankenstein* saga. Aside from a slightly im-

As Cauchon in his last Broadway stage production, *The Lark.*

pressive budget, the only interesting feature it had to offer was a brief closeup of the Monster at the end, revealing it to be Karloff himself. (Actually, six–foot–nine Mike Lane portrayed the Monster.) Karloff said:

> . . . I don't mind playing in another *Frankenstein* film because I have a sentimental attachment and a sorrow for the things done to the poor Monster in the other pictures which I didn't appear in . . . I feel I owe him a debt of gratitude and affection. . . . A man would be a fool if he turned his back on the thing that changed his life.

After the film was completed, he concentrated solely on video for the next five years. He also did a radio program for *Reader's Digest,* and made many spoken recordings of children's stories. He said:

> TV has released me completely from the shadow of the Monster. I play all manner of characters on television—things they would never allow me to do in films. Most of my parts are dramatic, to be sure. But I'm no longer thought of as a "heavy." I even sang and danced on Donald O'Connor's show. Can you imagine the movies letting me carry on like that?

In 1960, he signed up to become the host of the "Thriller" video series. He also appeared in five of the hour–long episodes.

He expressed criticism for contemporary screen shockers:

> There's so much needless violence, horror pictures have become ludicrous. Audiences are amused instead of frightened. Terror is the key, not bloodshed and fights. There was very little violence in *Frankenstein.* The Monster was gentle and a sympathetic character. . . . There is no compassion for today's monsters because they have no basis in reality. Instead they borrow liberally from the old pictures, but infuse no real story in the bargain. They just time the violence to perk things up when the story begins to slow up. They're not what they used to be.

In early 1963, Karloff signed a multi–film con-

With Elke Sommer on the set of *The Venetian Affair.*

tract with American International Pictures. The studio had achieved a reputation for low–budget science–fiction and horror films like *I Was a Teenage Werewolf,* and had advanced to elaborate color productions. Using Vincent Price and former stars Basil Rathbone and Peter Lorre in Poe adaptations, they emerged as the sole U. S. company to rival Hammer Films in shockers. Establishing proof of the aging actor's drawing power, the studio inserted clauses in his contract restricting his services concerning horror films exclusively to AIP. His first film was *The Raven,* which was not a remake of his old Universal classic, but an original story by Richard Matheson. In this large–scale Poe spoof, he played an evil magician who turns Peter Lorre into a raven. The purists deplored the humorous distortions of Poe's poem, but the film reaped even more profits than its predecessors. Its director Roger Corman, immediately cast him in a quickie, *The Terror,* ingeniously utilizing the still–standing sets of *The Raven.*

Though well past the age of retirement, he refused to do so. "If I did, I'd be dead within a few months," he said, "I intend to die with my boots, and my grease paint, on." Other AIP efforts followed, among them *Comedy of Terrors* and *Die, Monster, Die*. In *Black Sabbath,* he added a vampire characterization to his list of macabre characterizations. But his most offbeat role during this period was in *Targets*. He effectively portrayed an aging horror star, Byron Orlok who is too tired and disillusioned with the Hollywood system to continue. His performance in this timely film (reminiscent of the Whitman killings in Texas) revealed the extent which the senseless violence of reality outshocks anything on the screen. The film was an appropriate climax to a long cinematic career. Upon its release, he said, "It's a very timely movie. The violence in this country is appalling. This country is very close to frontier life. Sometimes we forget that."

During these latter years, his physical condition started to decline. Because of arthritis, he was forced to rely on a cane and to wear a metal brace on his leg. He also was suffering from affected lungs. While making *The Crimson Cult* in England, he contracted a serious case of pneumonia and was confined to a wheelchair throughout the filming. After he completed another film in Spain, he signed up for a series of Mexican films. But his doctor forbade him to go to Mexico City, because

of the altitude. With an oxygen tank nearby, his scenes were shot in Hollywood instead. The producer was instructed to place his $400,000 salary in a Mexican bank, but Karloff did not live long enough to collect it.

Following the completion of a TV episode "The Name of the Game," he caught a severe chill while returning to England. He was admitted to King Edward VII Hospital in Midhurst, Sussex. Several months later, he died of a respiratory ailment on February 2, 1969. He was 81. His friends believed that his life could have been lengthened if he slowed down a bit, but the Grand Old Man of Horror refused to be separated from the craft he loved.

Once asked whether he regretted having his career "typed" due to his association with Frankenstein's Monster, the actor replied:

One always hears of actors complaining of being typed—if he's young, he's typed as a juvenile; if he's handsome, he's typed as a leading man. I was lucky. Whereas bootmakers have to spend millions to establish a trademark, I was handed a trademark free of charge. When an actor gets in a position to select his own roles, he's in big trouble, for he never knows what he can do best. I'm sure I'd be damn good as little Lord Fauntleroy, but who would pay ten cents to see it?

Chatting with visitors on the set of his Mexican films in 1968.

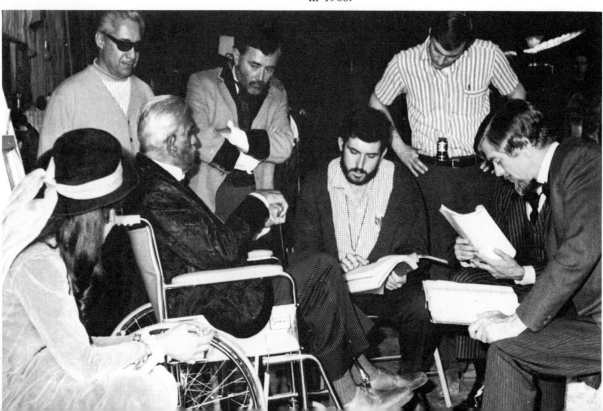

The FILMS of
BORIS KARLOFF

As an evil half-breed in *The Cave Girl*.

Early Films

Silent Films

HIS MAJESTY, THE AMERICAN
United Artists   1919.

Directed by Joseph Henabery. *Screenplay by* Henabery *and* "Elton Thomas" (pseudonym of Douglas Fairbanks). With Douglas Fairbanks, Lillian Langton, Frank Campeau, Sam Southern and Marjorie Daw.

Karloff was an extra in this adventure story.

THE PRINCE AND BETTY
Pathé   1919.

Directed by Robert Thornby. With William Desmond and Mary Thurman.

Karloff had a small role in this production, set in the mythical kingdom of Mervo.

THE DEADLIER SEX
Pathé   1920.

Directed by Robert Thornby. With Blanche Sweet and Mahlon Hamilton.

In his first noticeable role, Karloff was Jules Borney, a villainous French–Canadian trapper.

THE COURAGE OF MARGE O'DOONE
Vitagraph   1920.

Directed by David Smith. *Screenplay by* Robert North Bradbury, *based on* James Oliver Curwood's *novel.* With Pauline Starke, Jack Curtis, Niles Welch and William Dyer.

Karloff played another "North Woods" trapper.

THE LAST OF THE MOHICANS
Associated Producers   1920.

Directed by Maurice Tourneur. *Screenplay by* Robert Dillon, *based on* James Fenimore Cooper's *novel.* With Wallace Beery, Barbara Bedford, Lillian Hall and Harry Lorraine.

Karloff had a small role as a marauding Indian.

WITHOUT BENEFIT OF CLERGY
Pathé   1921.

Directed by James Young. *Based on a story by* Rudyard Kipling. With Virginia Brown Faire and Thomas Holding.

Karloff played the major menace, Ahmed Khan.

With William Desmond (Center) in *The Prince and Betty*.

THE HOPE DIAMOND MYSTERY
Kosmik   1921.

Fifteen–Chapter serial. *Directed by* Stuart Payton. *Screenplay by* Charles Goddard *and* John B. Clymer, *based on stories by* May Yohe. With Grace Darmond.

Karloff played Dakar, a Hindu servant.

CHEATED HEARTS
Universal   1921.

Directed by Hobart Henley. *Screenplay by* Wallace Clifton, *based on a story by* William Payson. With Herbert Rawlinson, Warner Baxter and Marjorie Daw.

Karloff played an Arab, Nei Hamid.

THE CAVE GIRL
First National   1922.

Directed by Joseph J. Franz. *Screenplay by* William Parker, *based on a play by* Guy Bolton *and* George Middleton. With Teddie Gerard, Charles Meredith, Wilton Taylor and Eleanor Hancock.

As a wicked half-breed, Karloff abducts the heroine. The film was shot in Yosemite Valley State Park.

THE MAN FROM DOWNING STREET
Vitagraph   1922.

Directed by Edward Jose. *Screenplay by* Bradley J. Smollen. With Earle Williams and Betty Ross Clarke.

Karloff played a maharajah in a melodrama about jewel thieves.

THE INFIDEL
First National   1922.

Directed by James Young. *Screenplay by* James Young. With Katherine MacDonald and Robert Ellis.

Karloff portrayed a murderous ruler of an island named Menang.

THE ALTAR STAIRS
Universal   1922.

Directed by Lambert Hillyer. *Screenplay by* Doris Schroeder, *based on a story by* G. B. Lancaster. With Frank Mayo and Louise Lorraine.

A South Seas melodrama, in which Karloff played a character named Hugo.

With an unidentified actor (Right) in the serial, *The Hope Diamond Mystery.*

OMAR THE TENTMAKER
First National   1922.

Directed by James Young. *Screenplay by* Richard Walton Tully, *based on his play,* "Omar Khayyam the Tentmaker." With Guy Bates Post, Virginia Brown Faire, Patsy Ruth Miller and Noah Beery.

Karloff played Iman, his first sympathetic role.

A WOMAN CONQUERS
First National   1923.

Directed by Tom Forman. *Based on a story by* Violet Clark. With Katherine MacDonald and Bryant Washburn.

In this outdoor adventure melodrama, Karloff played another French–Canadian.

THE PRISONER
Universal   1923.

Directed by Jack Conway. *Based on the novel* "Castle Craneycrow" *by* George Barr McCutcheon. With Herbert Rawlinson.

Karloff had a minor role in this Graustarkian melodrama.

THE HELLION
Sunset   1924.

Directed by Bruce Mitchell. *Screenplay by* Bruce Mitchell. With J. B. Warner and Marin Sais.

In this minor western, Karloff played an outlaw.

DYNAMITE DAN
Sunset   1924.

Directed by Bruce Mitchell. *Screenplay by* Bruce Mitchell. With Kenneth MacDonald and Frank Rice.

Karloff was a villain in this boxing comedy–melodrama.

PARISIAN NIGHTS
F.B.O.   1925.

Directed by Alfred Santell. *Screenplay by* Fred Myton *and* Doty Hobart, *based on a story by* Emile Forst. With Elaine Hammerstein, Renée Adorée and Lou Tellegen.

Karloff played a sadistic Parisian apache.

FORBIDDEN CARGO
F.B.O.   1925.

Directed by Tom Buckingham. *Screenplay by* Frederick Myton. With Evelyn Brent and Robert Ellis.

Karloff played the wicked mate of a rum-running ship.

THE PRAIRIE WIFE
Metro-Goldwyn 1925.

Directed by Hugo Ballin. With Dorothy Devore, Herbert Rawlinson and Gibson Gowland.

Karloff played a Mexican half-breed in this western.

LADY ROBIN HOOD
F.B.O. 1925.

Directed by Ralph Ince. *Based on a story by* Clifford Howard *and* Burke Jenkins. With Evelyn Brent and Robert Ellis.

Karloff portrayed Cabraza, henchman of the evil governor.

NEVER THE TWAIN SHALL MEET
Metro-Goldwyn 1925.

Directed by Maurice Tourneur. *Screenplay by* Eugene Mullin, *based on a story by* Peter B. Kyne. With Anita Stewart, Bert Lytell and Huntly Gordon.

Karloff had a minor role in this South Sea Island melodrama.

THE GREATER GLORY
First National 1926.

Directed by Curt Rehfeld. *Screenplay by* June Mathis, *based on the novel* "Viennese Medley" *by* Edith O'Shaughnessy. With Anna Q. Nillson, Conway Tearle, Jean Hersholt and Ian Keith.

In this drama of World War I Vienna, Karloff was barely noticeable.

HER HONOR, THE GOVERNOR
F.B.O. 1926.

Directed by Chet Withey. *Screenplay by* Doris Anderson, *based on a story by* Hyatt Daab *and* Weed Dickinson. With Pauline Frederick, Tom Santschi and Carroll Nye.

Karloff played Snipe Collins in this political melodrama. His performance as a drug addict was singled out for praise in *The New York Times*.

THE NICKLEHOPPER
Pathé 1926.

Directed by F. Richard Jones. With Mabel Normand, Michael Visaroff, Margaret Seddon, Theodore von Eltz, James Finlayson and Oliver Hardy.

In this Hal Roach–produced short, Karloff

In a typical villainous role (Right) in an unidentified film during the mid-twenties.

played a masher who tries to molest Mabel Normand.

THE BELLS
Chadwick 1926.

Directed by James Young. *Screenplay by* Young, *based on the play by* Erckmann–Chatrian. With Lionel Barrymore, Lola Todd, Gustav von Seyffertitz, Edward Phillips, Caroline Frances Cooke, Lorimer Johnson and Lucille LaVerne.

Karloff's most important role up till that time, as a side–show mesmerist who breaks down the murderer (Barrymore).

EAGLE OF THE SEA
Paramount 1926.

Directed by Frank Lloyd. *Screenplay by* Julian Josephson. With Ricardo Cortez and Florence Vidor.

Karloff played a member of Jean Lafitte's pirate crew.

FLAMES
Associated Exhibitors 1926.

Directed by Lewis Moomaw. *Screenplay by* Alfred A. Cohn. With Eugene O'Brien, Virginia Valli, Jean Hersholt and Bryant Washburn.

Karloff played a railroad bandit.

THE GOLDEN WEB
Gotham   1926.

Directed by Walter Lang. *Screenplay by* James Bell Smith, *based on the novel by* E. Phillips Oppenheim. With Lillian Rich and Huntly Gordon.

Karloff played one of the victims in this murder thriller.

FLAMING FURY
F.B.O.   1926.

Directed by James Hogan. *Based on a story by* Ewart Adamson. With Charles Delaney.

Karloff was Gaspard, a villainous French–Canadian.

VALENCIA
MGM   1926.

Directed by Dimitri Buchowetzki. *Screenplay by* Alice D. G. Miller. With Mae Murray, Lloyd Hughes and Roy D'Arcy.

Karloff had an unbilled role in this romantic melodrama, set in Barcelona.

MAN IN THE SADDLE
Universal   1926.

Directed by Clifford S. Smith. *Screenplay by* Charles A. Logue. With Hoot Gibson and Virginia Brown Faire.

Karloff portrayed a villain in this western melodrama.

OLD IRONSIDES
Paramount   1926.

Directed by James Cruze. *Based on a novel by* Lawrence Stallings. With Charles Farrell, Esther Ralston, Wallace Beery and George Bancroft.

Karloff was a Barbary pirate in another sea saga.

TARZAN AND THE GOLDEN LION
F.B.O.   1927.

Directed by J. P. McGowan. *Screenplay by* William E. Wing, *based on the novel by* Edgar Rice Burroughs. With James Pierce, Dorothy Dunbar, Edna Murphy, Harold Goodwin and Fred Peters.

In this penultimate silent Tarzan film, Karloff played the chief of the Waziri tribe.

With Evelyn Brent in *Lady Robin Hood*.

As the Mesmerist in *The Bells*.

LET IT RAIN
    Paramount   1927.

Directed by Eddie Cline. *Screenplay by* Wade Boteler, George J. Crone *and* Earle Snell. With Douglas MacLean, Shirley Mason and Wade Boteler.

Karloff was a minor villain in this U. S. Marine comedy.

THE MEDDLIN' STRANGER
    Pathé   1927.

Directed by Richard Thorpe. *Screenplay by* Christopher B. Booth. With Wally Wales.

A western in which Karloff was one of the principal villains.

42

With Douglas MacLean (Center) in *Soft Cushions*.

PRINCESS FROM HOBOKEN
    Tiffany   1927.

Directed by Allan Dale. *Screenplay by* Sonya Levien. With Blanche Mehaffey, Edmund Burns and Lou Tellegen.
    Karloff had a minor role in this comedy–drama.

PHANTOM BUSTER
    Pathé   1927.

Directed by William Bertram. *Screenplay by* Betty Burbridge. With Buddy Roosevelt.
    Karloff portrayed Ramon, a border smuggler.

With Louis Wolheim (Left) and William Boyd in *Two Arabian Knights*.

43

With Billie Dove in *The Love Mart*.

SOFT CUSHIONS
 Paramount   1927.

Directed by Eddie Cline. *Screenplay by* Wade Boteler *and* Frederik Chapin, *based on a story by* George Randolph Chester. With Douglas Mac-Lean, Sue Carol, Richard Carle and Frank Leigh.

In this Arabian Nights comedy, Karloff was the principal conspirator.

TWO ARABIAN KNIGHTS
 UA–Howard Hughes   1927.

Directed by Lewis Milestone. *Screenplay by* James O'Donohue, Wallace Smith *and* Cyril Gardner. With William Boyd, Louis Wolheim, Mary Astor and Ian Keith.

Karloff had a minor role in this army life comedy which was the first film to win an Academy Award for its direction.

THE LOVE MART
 First National   1928.

Directed by George Fitzmaurice. *Screenplay by* Benjamin Glazer, *based on the novel by* Edward Childs Carpenter. With Billie Dove, Gilbert Roland and Noah Beery.

Karloff played a villain in this lavishly produced melodrama of old New Orleans.

BURNING THE WIND
 Universal   1928.

Directed by Henry MacRae *and* Herbert Blanche. *Based on the novel* "A Daughter of the Dons" *by* William MacLeod Raine. With Hoot Gibson and Virginia Brown Faire.

Karloff was a ranch foreman who kidnapped the heroine.

VULTURES OF THE SEA
 Mascot   1928.   Ten–chapter serial.

Directed by Richard Thorpe. With Johnny Walker, Shirley Mason and Tom Santschi.

LITTLE WILD GIRL
 Trinity   1929.

Directed by Frank Mattison. *Screenplay by* Cecil B. Hill, *based on a story by* Putnam Hoover. With Lila Lee, Cullen Landis and Frank Merrill.

Again Karloff was a villain in this "North Woods" melodrama.

With Warner Baxter in *Behind That Curtain*.

THE DEVIL'S CHAPLAIN
Rayart   1929.

Directed by Duke Worne. *Screenplay by* Arthur Hoerl, *based on a story by* George Bronson Howard. With Cornelius Keefe, Virginia Brown Faire and Joseph Swickard.

A spy melodrama in which Karloff was barely noticeable.

THE FATAL WARNING
Mascot   1929.   Ten–chapter serial.

Directed by Richard Thorpe. With Helene Costello, Ralph Graves and Syd Crossley.

TWO SISTERS
Rayart   1929.

Directed by Scott Pembroke. *Screenplay by* Arthur Hoerl, *based on a story by* Virginia T. Vandewater. With Viola Dana, Rex Lease, Claire Dubrey, Irving Bacon and Tom Lingham.

Karloff played Viola Dana's henchman.

PHANTOMS OF THE NORTH
Biltmore   1929.

Directed by Henry Webb. *Screenplay by* George Hull *and* Carl Kursada, *based on a story by* Flora E. Douglas. With Edith Roberts, Donald Keith and Joe Bonomo.

Karloff was a "North Woods" villain for the last time.

ANNE AGAINST THE WORLD
Rayart   1929.

Directed by Duke Worne. *Screenplay by* Arthur Hoerl, *based on a story by* Victor Thorne. With Shirley Mason, Jack Mower, James Bradbury Jr. and Isabel Keith.

Karloff had a minor role in this show–business melodrama.

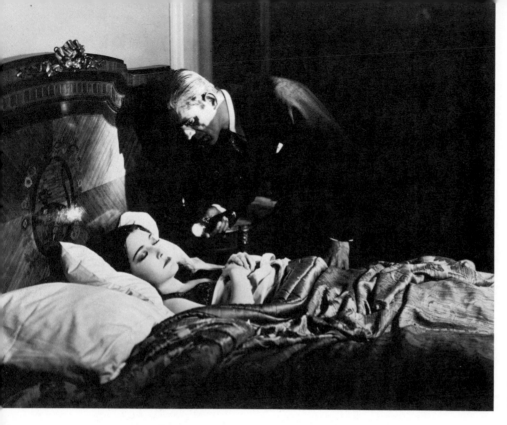

With Dorothy Sebastian in
The Unholy Night.

Sound Films

BEHIND THAT CURTAIN
    Fox   1929.

*Released in both silent and sound versions.
Directed by* Irving Cummings. *Screenplay by*
Sonya Levien *and* Clarke Silvernail, *based on the
novel by* Earl Derr Biggers. With Warner Baxter,
Lois Moran, Claude King, E. A. Park and Gilbert Emery.

In this first Charlie Chan talkie, Karloff's role
was nearly as minor as the Chan role.

KING OF THE KONGO
    Mascot   1929.   Ten–chapter serial.

*Released in both silent and part–talking
versions.*
Directed by Richard Thorpe. With Jacqueline
Logan, Walter Miller and Richard Tucker.

In this jungle adventure, Karloff played Scarface Macklin, leader of a gang.

With Richard Dix in *The Public
Defender.*

As a bandit in *The Utah Kid*.

As Ned Galloway in *The Criminal Code*.

THE UNHOLY NIGHT
MGM   1929.

Released in both silent and sound versions. Directed by Lionel Barrymore. *Screenplay by* Dorothy Farnum *and* Edwin Justus Mayer, *based on a story by* Ben Hecht. With Ernest Torrence, Dorothy Sebastian, Roland Young, Natalie Moorhead, Polly Moran, Sojin and John Loder.

In this murder mystery set in England, Karloff played a mysterious Hindu servant.

THE BAD ONE
United Artists   1930.

Directed by George Fitzmaurice. *Screenplay by* John Farrow, Carey Wilson *and* Howard Emmett Rogers. With Dolores Del Rio, Edmund Lowe, Don Alvarado and Ulrich Haupt.

Karloff portrayed a guard in a penal colony.

THE SEA BAT
MGM   1930.

Directed by Wesley Ruggles. *Screenplay by* Bess Meredyth *and* John Howard Lawson, *based on a story by* Dorothy Yost. With Raquel Torres, Charles Bickford, Nils Asther, George F. Marion, John Miljan and Gibson Gowland.

Karloff again played an evil half-breed.

THE UTAH KID
Tiffany   1930.

Directed by Richard Thorpe. *Screenplay by* Frank Howard Clark. With Rex Lease, Dorothy Sebastian, Tom Santschi, Mary Carr and Walter Miller.

Karloff played a bandit in his last western.

MOTHERS CRY
First National   1930.

Directed by Hobart Henley. *Screenplay by* Lenore J. Coffee, *based on the novel by* Helen Grace Carlisle. With Dorothy Peterson, Helen Chandler, David Manners and Edward Woods.

Karloff was a murder victim.

THE CRIMINAL CODE
Columbia   1931.

Directed by Howard Hawks. *Screenplay by* Fred

Niblo Jr. *and* Seton I. Miller, *based on the play by* Martin Flavin. With Walter Huston, Phillips Holmes, Constance Cummings, Mary Doran, De-Witt Jennings and John Sheehan.

In this filming of the famous play, Karloff repeated his stage role of Ned Galloway, convict trusty turned killer. His performance brought him to the attention of other producers, who cast him in more important films.

CRACKED NUTS
RKO Radio   1931.

Directed by Edward Cline. *Screenplay by* Al Boasberg. With Wheeler and Woolsey, Edna May Oliver, Louis Calhern, Dorothy Lee, Leni Stengel and Stanley Fields.

Karloff had a minor role of a revolutionary in this comedy, located in the mythical kingdom of El Dorania.

YOUNG DONOVAN'S KID
RKO Radio   1931.

Directed by Fred Niblo. *Screenplay by* J. Walter Ruben, *based on the story* "Big Brother" *by* Rex Beach. With Richard Dix, Marion Shilling, Jackie Cooper and Frank Sheridan.

Karloff played a drug pusher who tried to corrupt young Jackie Cooper.

KING OF THE WILD
Mascot   1931.   Twelve–chapter serial.

Directed by Richard Thorpe. *Screenplay by* Wyndham Gittens *and* Ford Beebe. With Walter Miller, Nora Lane, Dorothy Christy, Tom Santschi, Victor Potel, Carroll Nye and Arthur McLaglen.

In his fifth and last serial, Karloff portrayed a villainous sheik.

SMART MONEY
Warner Bros.   1931.

Directed by Alfred E. Green. *Screenplay by* Kubec Glasmon, John Bright, Lucien Hubbard *and* Joseph Jackson. With Edward G. Robinson, James Cagney, Evelyn Knapp, Noel Francis and Morgan Wallace.

Karloff played a crooked gambler who tried to cheat Robinson.

THE PUBLIC DEFENDER
RKO Radio   1931.

Directed by J. Walter Ruben. *Screenplay by* Bernard Schubert, *based on the novel by* George Goodschild. With Richard Dix. Shirley Grey, Paul Hurst, Edmund Breese, Purnell Pratt and Ruth Weston.

In a crime melodrama, Karloff played The Professor, Dix's cultured accomplice.

I LIKE YOUR NERVE
Warner Bros.   1931.

Directed by William McGann. *Screenplay by* Houston Branch, *based on a story by* Roland Pertwee. With Douglas Fairbanks Jr., Loretta Young, Edmund Breon, Henry Kolker, Claude Allister, Ivan Simpson and Paul Porcasi.

Karloff had a small role as a butler in this south–of–the–border comedy–adventure.

PARDON US
(*French foreign–language version*)
Roach–MGM   1931.

Directed by James Parrott. *Screenplay by* H. M. Walker. With Stanley Laurel, Oliver Hardy, June Marlowe, Guido Trento, James Finlayson and Walter Long.

Karloff played a convict who menaces Laurel and Hardy.

With Oliver Hardy and Stanley Laurel in the French–language version of *Pardon Us*.

With Dorothy Revier.

Christy Cabanne (wearing moustache behind camera) directs Karloff and Regis Toomey.

Graft

Universal   1931.

CREDITS

Directed by Christy Cabanne. *Screenplay by* Barry Barringer. *Photography,* Jerome Ash. *Editor,* Maurice Pivar. Released September 21, 1931. Running time: 54 minutes.

CAST

Regis Toomey, Sue Carol, Dorothy Revier, Boris Karloff, George Irving, William Davidson, Richard Tucker, Willard Robertson, Harold Goodwin and Carmelita Geraghty.

SYNOPSIS

Dusty (Regis Toomey), a young cub reporter on a big–city newspaper, is determined to bring in a big story on his own. In the forthcoming city election, a crooked politician learns Pearl (Dorothy Revier), his former mistress, is going to spill the beans to the District Attorney. Fearful of indictment, the politician orders the D.A. murdered and Pearl kidnapped. Dusty stumbles on the murder and erroneously accuses Constance (Sue Carol), the reform candidate's daughter, of the murder. After his story appears in the paper the next day, the editor fires Dusty.

Dusty trails the crooks and Pearl to a yacht, where she is being held prisoner. After a terrific battle, Dusty captures Terry, the leading henchman (Boris Karloff), and frees Pearl as the police arrive. The young reporter gets back to the newspaper in time to give them his story. Dusty not only gets his job back, but wins Constance's love.

REVIEW

Another newspaper story carrying on Hollywood's idea of what goes on around a city desk. Whole thing so dizzy and unreal it is almost funny. . . .
Variety

With Ona Munson, Edward G. Robinson and Aline MacMahon.

Five Star Final

Warner Bros.   1931.

CREDITS

Directed by Mervyn LeRoy, *Screenplay by* Robert Lord. *Based on the play by* Louis Weitzenkorn. *Photography,* Sol Polito. *Editor,* Frank Ware. Released September 26, 1931. Running time: 89 minutes.

CAST

Edward G. Robinson, H. B. Warner, Marian Marsh, Anthony Bushell, George E. Stone, Frances Starr, Ona Munson, Polly Walters, Robert Elliott, Aline MacMahon, Gladys Lloyd, Boris Karloff, Evelyn Hall, David Torrence, Harold Waldridge and Oscar Apfel.

SYNOPSIS

Bernard Hinchecliffe (Oscar Apfel) is the owner of the notorious scandal sheet, the *Gazette*. His managing editor, Joseph Randall (Edward G. Robinson), is ordered to boost the circulation by doing a series of articles on the Vorhees case. Years before, Nancy Vorhees (Frances Starr) murdered the man who betrayed her. Now remarried as Mrs. Townsend, her daughter Jenny (Marian Marsh) is about to be married to young Phillip Weeks (Anthony Bushell). Randall enlists the services of T. Vernon Isopod (Boris Karloff), an expelled divinity student. Isopod disguises himself as a clergyman and· enters the

Townsend home. Gaining their confidence, he learns of the impending marriage and is permitted to take photos.

After the first *Gazette* article appears on the morning of the wedding, Nancy and her husband commit suicide. Weeks' mother refuses to let the young couple marry. Hysterical, Jenny goes to the newspaper to shoot Hinchecliffe. But Phillip stops her and threatens to kill the publisher himself if the articles continue. Ashamed of his part in the tragedy, Randall tells off Hinchecliffe and resigns.

NOTES

The author of the original play, Louis Weitzenkorn, was once the managing editor of the New York *Evening Graphic,* a wildly sensationalistic tabloid. He left in indignation and wrote the play. The character of Hinchecliffe supposedly resembled the publisher of the *New York Mirror. Film Daily* chose this film as one of the ten best of 1931. The film was remade as *Two Against The World* by the same studio in 1936.

REVIEWS

The stage success . . . has been brought to the screen as a smashing drama with plenty of punch. . . . The patrons pronounced it crackerjack entertainment.

Motion Picture Herald

All the necessary ingredients for a box–office picture are in this one, although they're treated in a radically different manner. . . . Ona Munson, Boris Karloff, Robert Elliott . . . carry their assignments perfectly . . . *Five Star Final* has no weak spots.

Variety

With Edward G. Robinson.

As Fedor's brutal father.

The Mad Genius

Warner Bros.   1931.

CREDITS

Directed by Michael Curtiz. *Screenplay by* J. Grubb Alexander *and* Harvey Thew. *Based on the play* The Idol *by* Martin Brown. *Photography,* Barney McGill. *Editor,* Ralph Dawson. *Ballet sequences by* Adolph Bolm. Released November 7, 1931. Running time: 81 minutes.

CAST

John Barrymore, Marian Marsh, Donald Cook, Carmel Meyers, Charles Butterworth, Luis Alberni, Andre Luget, Boris Karloff, Frankie Darro and Mae Madison.

SYNOPSIS

Tsarakov (John Barrymore) is a crippled, half–mad puppeteer, who yearns to dance. Upon rescuing a young boy Fedor (Frankie Darro) from his foster father's (Boris Karloff) abuse, he recognizes the youth's natural agility. Fired with ambition, Tsarakov raises him to manhood hoping to make him a famous dancer. The puppeteer becomes the impresario of a successful ballet com-

pany. His most promising dancers are Fedor (Donald Cook) and a young girl, Nana Carolova (Marian Marsh). The ballet master is Serge Bankieff (Luis Alberni), a drug addict. Discovering that Fedor and Nana have fallen in love, Tsarakov tries to separate them. But they leave the company and go to Paris. Realizing she is interfering with Fedor's future, Nana leaves him.

After returning to Tsarakov's company, Fedor eventually becomes a great dancer. During a performance, Fedor sees Nana in the audience. The young man weakens, but his master's uncanny hold on him is too strong. Before the ballet's completion, Bankieff, crazed with an overdose of drugs, kills Tsarakov with an axe. Fedor discovers the mutilated body of his master on the stage. Freed from his influence, Fedor is finally reunited with Nana.

NOTES

The film, based on an unproduced play, was derived from two sources: the life of Nijinsky and

54

With John Barrymore.

Du Maurier's novel *Trilby*. The latter was recently filmed as *Svengali,* by the same studio. It starred Barrymore and Marian Marsh. Inspired by its box–office success and story similarity, Warners produced *The Mad Genius,* using the same star and leading lady.

Karloff's role was minor, and did not reapppear after the opening sequence. The following mention of *Frankenstein* in the dialogue may be a mere coincidence: "Have you heard of the Golem, fashioned from mud and given a human soul?" asks Tsarakov. "Frankenstein's man? Homunculus, the product of science? They were dreams brought to life by mortals, and if they can—I will create my Golem, my Frankenstein man. That boy shall be my counterpart, the thing I should have been. . . ."

REVIEW

Although the story . . . is interesting while Mr. Barrymore occupies the screen, it becomes numb once he disappears. Sometimes it recalls Mrs. Shelley's *Frankenstein,* but as a whole it is more like . . . *Trilby.*

. . . The director deserves a great deal of credit for his share of the work and it is a pity that he did not have the power to order some of the dialogue changed and also to have something to say concerning the selection of the players.

Mordaunt Hall, *The New York Times*

With Elissa Landi.

The Yellow Ticket

Fox   1931.

CREDITS

Directed by Raoul Walsh. *Screenplay by* Jules Furthman *and* Guy Bolton. *Based on the play by* Michael Morton. *Photography,* James Wong Howe. *Editor,* Jack Murray. Released November 15, 1931. Running time: 76 minutes.

CAST

Elissa Landi, Lionel Barrymore, Laurence Olivier, Walter Byron, Sarah Padden, Arnold Korff, Mischa Auer, Boris Karloff and Rita La Roy.

SYNOPSIS

In 1913 Russia, Mary Kalish (Elissa Landi) a Jewish girl, learns that her father is dying in a St. Petersburg prison. Since Jews cannot travel without passports, she is forced to obtain a "yellow ticket," one issued to prostitutes. After she arrives, she learns that her father has died. Determined not to let her mother discover her ticket, she remains and finds work. There, she meets and falls in love with Julian Rolfe (Laurence Olivier), a British journalist. Shocked by her story, he writes a series of articles exposing conditions in the country.

Infuriated by these articles, Baron Andrey (Lionel Barrymore), head of the Czar's secret police, threatens to imprison her lover. After he tries to seduce her, she kills him. Taking advantage of the Austrian invasion of Russia, the young couple escapes to England.

NOTES

In his third film association with Lionel Barrymore, Karloff had the small role of his drunken orderly who tries to molest Landi in a public park. The plot was obviously derived from the opera *Tosca*.

REVIEW

An estimable antiquity, full of perils for Elissa Landi . . . [a] grim but lively melodrama . . . Barrymore, the best leerer in his family, achieves facial contortions of unparalleled eloquence.

Time

With Elliott Rothe and Leo Carrillo.

Guilty Generation

Columbia   1931.

CREDITS

Directed by Rowland V. Lee. *Screenplay by* Jack Cunningham. *Based on the play by* Jo Milward *and* J. Kirby Hawkes. *Photography,* Byron Haskin. *Editor,* Otis Garrett. Released November 19, 1931. Running time: 82 minutes.

CAST

Leo Carrillo, Constance Cummings, Robert Young, Boris Karloff, Emma Dunn, Leslie Fenton, Ruth Warren, Murray Kinnell and Elliott Rothe.

SYNOPSIS

Two notorious gangsters, Mike Palmero (Leo Carrillo) and Tony Ricca (Boris Karloff), are fighting for control of the bootlegging racket. Maria (Constance Cummings), Palmero's daughter, fears him and hates his criminal activities. She falls in love with Ricca's son, Marco (Robert Young). As the gang war continues, there are further deaths. Fearful that her father will kill Marco, Maria keeps their love a secret.

Discovering that Marco and Maria have married, Mike Palmero orders the young man's death. But his mother kills Mike and ends further bloodshed.

REVIEW

. . . A lively gang picture . . . Critics wondered whether *Hamlet* wouldn't make a better gangster plot than *Romeo and Juliet.*

Time

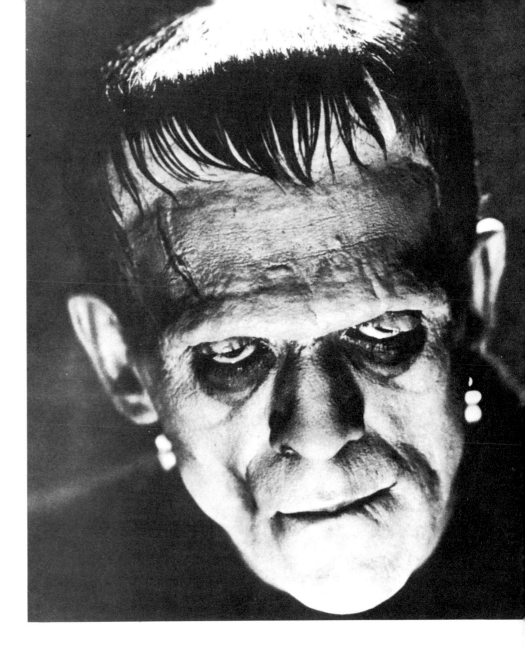

Frankenstein

Universal   1931.

CREDITS

Directed by James Whale. *Produced by* Carl Laemmle Jr. *Screenplay by* Garrett Fort *and* Francis Faragoh. *Adapted by* John L. Balderston *from the play by* Peggy Webling. *Based on the novel by* Mary Wollstonecraft Shelley. *Photography,* Arthur Edeson. *Editor,* Maurice Pivar. *Makeup,* Jack Pierce. Released November 21, 1931. Running time: 71 minutes.

CAST

Colin Clive, Mae Clarke, John Boles, Boris Karloff, Edward Van Sloan, Dwight Frye, Frederick Kerr, Lionel Belmore, Michael Mark and Marilyn Harris.

SYNOPSIS

Henry Frankenstein (Colin Clive), a scientist, is obsessed with ambition to create life artificially.

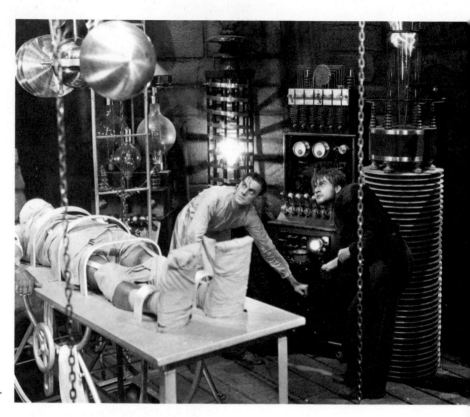

With Colin Clive and Dwight Frye.

Aided by Fritz (Dwight Frye), a hunchbacked dwarf, he steals bodies from cemeteries to supply parts for his creation. Instructed to steal a brain from a medical college, Fritz mistakenly obtains a criminal brain instead of a normal one. Alarmed over his condition, Elizabeth (Mae Clarke), his fiancee, Victor (John Boles), his best friend, and Dr. Waldman (Edward Van Sloan), Henry's old teacher, visit the abandoned watch tower where Frankenstein is experimenting in seclusion. While a storm rages outside, the young scientist harnesses its electrical energy and brings life to an inanimate creature (Boris Karloff).

Frankenstein's monstrous creation is kept in an old dungeon in the tower where Fritz torments him. Awakened to rage, the Monster strangles the dwarf. After great difficulty in subduing the creature, Henry suffers a nervous breakdown. While Frankenstein returns to his estate to recover his health, Dr. Waldman promises to destroy the creature. On Henry's wedding day, he learns the Monster has strangled Dr. Waldman and escaped. After drowning a peasant's daughter, the creature enters the house and terrorizes Elizabeth. The entire village is aroused. Young Frankenstein joins them in searching the countryside for the mur-

derer. Becoming separated from the others, Henry is overcome by the Monster and carried off to an old mill. There, Frankenstein and his creation battle on the roof. After the scientist is hurled to the ground, the villagers burn the mill to the ground, presumably destroying the creature. Frankenstein recovers and marries Elizabeth.

NOTES

Karloff's makeup man, Jack Pierce, died in 1968. The veteran repeated his chores on every horror film produced by this studio in the 1930s and continued in this capacity until 1947. The electrical machinery in the laboratory sequence was created and operated by Frank Grove, Kenneth Strickfaden and Raymond Lindsay.

This picture was important in several ways. Financially one of the most successful of the 1931–32 season, it showed the executives of Universal that this type of material could be accepted by audiences. Even more than *Dracula*, this picture set the pattern for Hollywood's subsequent treatment of the subject of horror. It was widely imitated, both at the time and in later years.

Actually, Mary Shelley's novel had been adapted to dramatic form as early as 1832. An actor

60

With Edward Van Sloan, Dwight Frye and Colin Clive.

named T. P. Cooke portrayed the Monster in this production at London's Theatre Royal. Its title was *Presumption: or, the Fate of Frankenstein,* and the author was R. B. Peake. Its success encouraged a musical spoof by Richard Henry and Meyer Lutz in 1887 at the Gaiety Theatre in the same city. In a prophetic anticipation of many contemporary parodies, the show featured vampires also: there was even a vampire ballet. In 1910, Thomas A. Edison produced the first film version, but no prints have survived. Miss Webling's play, opening in London on February 10, 1930, featured Hamilton Deane as the Monster.

Universal was uncertain of how to finish their screen adaptation of the 1930 play. Should the Monster and his creator die at the end, as they

With Marilyn Harris.

61

With Mae Clarke.

had on the stage? The studio filmed two endings, one happy, one unhappy. Following a preview, they decided to use the one in which the doctor lives. They also deleted the scene containing the murder of the little girl by the Monster, because of audience criticism.

When the film was revived in 1938, it proved nearly as successful as the first time. On a double bill with *Dracula,* it played to sell-out crowds in Salt Lake City, Waterbury, Connecticut, and other cities. In one city, a crowd of 4,000 broke into the theatre in their eagerness to see the picture. The enterprising manager promptly rented the theatre across the street—and filled it. This success story, on a more modest scale, was repeated through the years. The television sale in 1957 led directly to the new horror film cycle of the late 1950s.

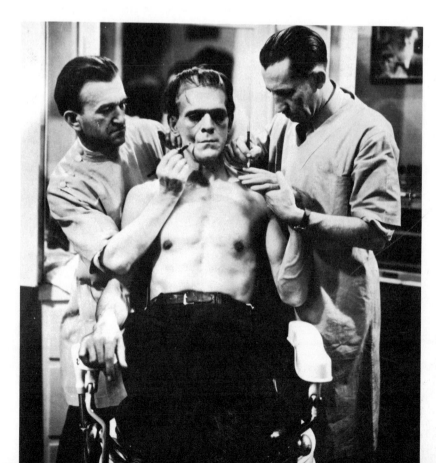

Makeup Man Jack Pierce (Left) transforms Karloff into the Frankenstein Monster.

REVIEWS

Out of . . . the Mary Shelley classic, *Frankenstein,* James Whale . . . has wrought a stirring Grand Guignol type of picture.

It is an artistically conceived work . . . naturally a morbid, gruesome affair, but it is something to keep the spectator awake, for during its most spine-chilling periods it exacts attention . . . Boris Karloff undertakes the Frankenstein creation and his makeup can be said to suit anybody's demands. . . .

No matter what one may say about the melodramatic ideas here, there is no denying that it is far and away the most effective thing of its kind. Beside it *Dracula* is tame. . . .

Mordaunt Hall, *The New York Times*

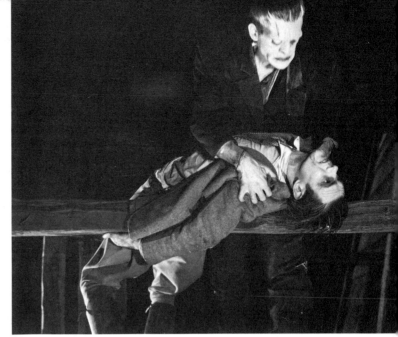

With Colin Clive.

If Universal's production of *Frankenstein* does nothing else, it establishes Boris Karloff as the one important candidate who has arisen for the mantle of the late Lon Chaney as a delineator of weird and grotesque roles. Because of his restraint, his intelligent simplicity of gesture, carriage, voice and makeup, Karloff has truly created a Frankenstein Monster. Had he yielded to the temptation to melodramatize as the opportunity offered, the character would have been far less formidable . . . Karloff has done some excellent

things in pictures, though usually in minor roles. This was his big opportunity, and whether you like the picture or not you won't deny his efficacy.

Frankenstein is a thriller, make no mistake. Women come out trembling, men exhausted. . . .

Leo Meehan, *Motion Picture Herald*

. . . *Frankenstein* isn't the ordinary tale of murder and mystery. It's a study of a chemical experiment—one which clutches at you icily and holds you until the romantic ending guarantees satisfaction after an hour's worth of gripping, intriguing horrors.

. . . James Whale directs the strange piece for the screen, proving once again that he's an ace megaphoner.

. . . The picture is skillfully worked out . . . in the Bavarian village where the plot is laid. It is absolutely real, never once smacking of papier mache. We believe in the endeavors of Henry (Clive) as a medical scientist to create life. And when a Monster, evolved by Henry's own hands . . . endowed with the human brain of a deceased criminal, actually breathes, grunts and walks, we're not in the least skeptical; merely fascinated. We know he's about to perform grotesque acts, and we don't question the plausibility of the tale . . . it is heartily interesting and wholly absorbing.

Irene Thirer, New York *Daily News*

Being photographed by Arthur Edeson on the set.

63

With Melvyn Douglas.

Tonight or Never

United Artists   1931.

CREDITS

Directed by Mervyn LeRoy. *Screenplay by* Ernest Vajda. *Adapted by* Frederick *and* Fanny Hatton *from the* David Belasco *stage play by* Lili Hatvany. *Photography,* Gregg Toland. *Editor,* Grant Whytlock. Released December 26, 1931. Running time: 82 minutes.

CAST

Gloria Swanson, Melvyn Douglas, Ferdinand Gottschalk, Robert Greig, Greta Mayer, Warburton Gamble, Alison Skipworth and Boris Karloff.

SYNOPSIS

Nella Vago (Gloria Swanson), a young singer, makes her operatic debut in Venice but discovers her reception disappointing. She learns from her teacher (Ferdinand Gottschalk) that her voice lacks warmth and feeling. While appearing there, a mysterious young man (Melvyn Douglas) follows her everywhere. Returning to her native Budapest, she learns a scout from the Metropolitan Opera refused to sign her until she truly feels her songs. Depressed, she goes to the young gigolo's apartment, where they make love. The following night, Nella surprises everyone by her marvelous performance in *Tosca*.

After the Met offers her a contract, she visits the gigolo's apartment and declares her love. Moved, he asks her to give up her profession and she tears up her contract. To her surprise, she discovers he is in reality Fletcher, a scout for the Met. The misunderstanding is over.

REVIEW

The cast—with the exception of Alison Skipworth, Gloria Swanson and Boris Karloff, Frankenstein's Monster, who herein plays a waiter—is the one which made the play a success in Manhattan where it was produced by the late David Belasco ... An easy-going, insignificant and funny cinematic escapade.

Time

With Jack Holt.

Behind the Mask

Columbia   1932.

CREDITS

Directed by John Francis Dillon. *Screenplay by* Jo Swerling *and* Dorothy Howell. *Based on the story* In the Secret Service *by* Jo Swerling. *Photography,* Ted Tetzlaff. *Editor,* Otis Garrett. Released February 25, 1932. Running time: 68 minutes.

CAST

Jack Holt, Constance Cummings, Boris Karloff, Claude King, Bertha Mann, Edward Van Sloan, Willard Robertson and Tommy Jackson.

SYNOPSIS

Dr. X, a mysterious master criminal, is the head of a dope ring. His identity is unknown even to his own men; any who succeed in penetrating his identity are killed. Investigating the gang, Jack Hart (Jack Holt), a Secret Service agent, wins the confidence of Henderson (Boris Karloff), a member of the gang. Through Henderson, Hart visits Arnold (Claude King), his superior, and joins the gang. A complication arises when he meets Arnold's daughter, Julie (Constance Cummings), and falls in love with her.

Shortly after, Arnold is killed by Dr. X because he talked too much. After Julie is kidnapped, Hart traces her to a private hospital run by Dr. Steiner (Edward Van Sloan). There, Hart's true identity is revealed and he is strapped to an operating table. Dr. Steiner appears and turns out to

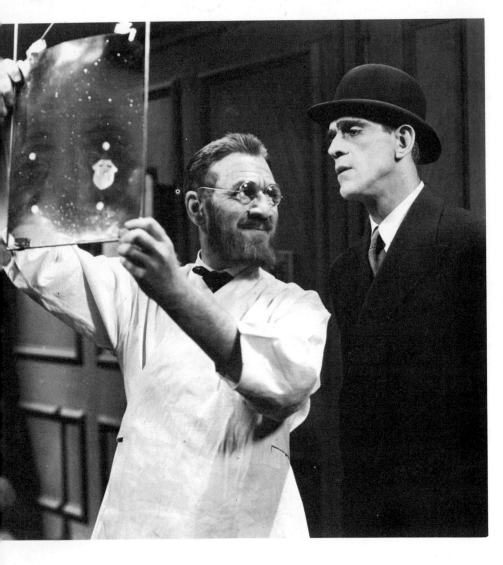

With Edward Van Sloan.

be Dr. X. Just as he is about to perform a fatal operation on Hart, he is shot by Julie.

NOTES

This film was made during the same period as *The Criminal Code* by the same studio. It borrowed its photographer and two cast members (Karloff and Miss Cummings) from the more expensive production. It also used some of the same sets and film footage. So that the similarities wouldn't be too obvious, its release was held up for a year. During this period, *Frankenstein* was released, and Columbia decided to play up Karloff's name and the picture's horror aspects in the advertising. But technically, it is not a horror film.

REVIEW

Exploited as another horror picture, this doesn't horrify sufficiently to class with preceding baby-scarers. But its virtues are a not–so–bad Secret Service story, well acted by a cast of veterans, and an inexpensive investment. . . .

The scare stuff seems tossed in regardless of where it fits, but it gets results . . . Karloff's threatening pan makes him a natural for his part.

"Bige," *Variety*

Will Rogers (wearing pith helmet).

Business and Pleasure

Fox   1932.

CREDITS

Directed by David Butler. *Screenplay by* William Conselman *and* Gene Towne. *From the play* The Plutocrat *by* Arthur Goodrich, *based on the novel by* Booth Tarkington. *Photography,* Ernest Palmer. Released March 6, 1932. Running time: 57 minutes.

CAST

Will Rogers, Jetta Goudal, Joel McCrea, Dorothy Peterson, Peggy Ross, Cyril Ring, Jed Prouty, Oscar Apfel, Vernon Dent and Boris Karloff.

SYNOPSIS

Earl Tinker (Will Rogers), a razor blade manufacturer, intends to obtain the secret of Damascus steel for his product. During a Mediterranean cruise with his family, he nearly falls into the clutches of attractive Madame Momora (Jetta Goudal), in the pay of his rival. Arriving in the desert, Tinker discovers his plans have leaked out and finds himself in the midst of a war between two Arab tribes.

After being captured by one of them, he saves himself from execution by faking a broadcast on a radio that was given to a sheik. Tinker discovers that tribal disputes are started when rival chiefs pull each others' beards. He stops the war by distributing his razor blades to them and wins his contract for Damascus steel.

NOTES

In this typical Will Rogers comedy, Karloff played a bearded desert chieftain. As his role was minor, he did not make his appearance until the last quarter of the film.

REVIEW

All the cast is quite adequate, but, as usual in Rogers pictures, this is pretty much all Will.

Motion Picture Herald

With unidentified extras.

Scarface

United Artists   1932.

CREDITS

Directed by Howard Hawks. *Produced by* Howard Hughes. *Screenplay by* Ben Hecht, Seton I. Miller, John Lee Mahin *and* W. R. Burnett. *Photography,* Lee Garmes *and* L. W. O'Connell. *Editor,* Edward Curtiss. Released March 26, 1932. Running time: 95 minutes.

CAST

Paul Muni, Ann Dvorak, Karen Morley, Osgood Perkins, Boris Karloff, C. Henry Gordon, George Raft, Purnell Pratt, Vince Barnett, Inez Palange, Harry J. Vejar, Edwin Maxwell, Tully Marshall, Henry Armetta and Bert Starkey.

SYNOPSIS

During prohibition, Johnny Lovo (Osgood Perkins), a Chicago gangster, moves in on the beer racket in his territory with the aide of a young hoodlum, Tony Camonte (Paul Muni). After Camonte assassinates Lovo's boss, Lovo gives him a second–in–command spot in his gang and a split in the profits. As the profits roll in, Tony's ambition grows. He soon covets Lovo's leadership and his mistress, Poppy (Karen Morley). While battling with rival gangs over control of the North Side, Camonte machine–guns Dorgan and his entire mob, including Gaffney (Boris Karloff), who is murdered in a bowling alley. Fearful of losing his position, Lovo arranges to have Tony taken for a ride. But Camonte escapes and orders his right–hand man Rinaldo (George Raft) to murder his boss.

After installing Poppy as his mistress, Tony becomes the undisputed underworld leader of the city. Discovering Rinaldo in love with his sister Cesca (Ann Dvorak), Tony shoots his best friend in a rage. Filled with revenge, Cesca reports the murder to the police and follows him to his hideout to kill him. Finding themselves surrounded by the police, Cesca instead joins her brother in battling them. After Cesca is killed, Tony becomes panic–stricken and is finally killed by police bullets.

NOTES

Scarface was adapted from Armitage Trail's novel, which was based on the career of Al Capone. But aside from several bloody incidents recreated from Chicago's crime–filled history like the killing of "Big Jim" Colosimo, the St. Valentine's Day Massacre and Dion O'Banion's execution in his flower shop, *Scarface* has nothing in common with Capone's life.

Completed in November 1931 after six months of shooting, Howard Hughes produced it on a lavish scale to make it the gangster picture to end all gangster pictures. But due to public out-rage at this new evil development of society, censors halted its release for months and forced Hughes to make his hero less sympathetic. This resulted in cuts making the continuity uneven and the insertion of scenes and titles containing moral preachments. Hughes was also pressured into making several endings for *Scarface*. One of them showed Camonte taking his place on the gallows, despite the fact that Chicago no longer uses it as its death penalty. But the censors still rejected it. Disgusted, Hughes decided to release it in almost original form.

By the time *Scarface* was finally released, the gangster cycle of films had run its course. How-ever, the film launched the careers of Paul Muni and especially George Raft, who was signed to a seven–year contract by Paramount.

REVIEWS

The slaughter in *Scarface* . . . is like that of a Shakespearean tragedy, for after the smoke of machine guns and pineapple bombs has blown away and the leading killer has gone to his death on the gallows, the only one . . . left is a blonde with carefully plucked eyebrows . . . the mistress of two underworld giants.

This pictorial recapitulation of the highlights of Chicago's recent history of crime . . . is a stirring picture, efficiently directed and capably acted. . . .

Boris Karloff appears as a rival gangster, but his British accent is hardly suitable to the role. . . .

The New York Times

Had *Scarface* been released a year or so ago it would have been hailed as a masterpiece of dra-matic realism by those who had never seen any-thing like it in the cinema before. But we've al-ready seen *Little Caesar* and *Public Enemy* . . . as a result . . . the edge has been somewhat taken off gangster shockers.

That there have been censorial eliminations is apparent from the faulty synchronization in the sequences cut.

New York Evening Journal

As Gaffney in the famous bowling alley massacre sequence.

With Sidney Fox, Lew Ayres and Genevieve Tobin.

The Cohens and Kellys in Hollywood

Universal   1932.

CREDITS

Directed by John Francis Dillon. *Screenplay by* Howard J. Green. *Photography,* Jerome Ash. *Editor,* Harry Webb. Released March 28, 1932. Running time: 75 minutes.

CAST

George Sidney, Charlie Murray, June Clyde, Norman Foster, Emma Dunn, Esther Howard, Eileen Percy, Edwin Maxwell, Dorothy Christy, Luis Alberni, John Roche, Robert Greig, Tom Mix, Lew Ayres, Sidney Fox, Boris Karloff, Genevieve Tobin and Harry Barris.

SYNOPSIS

Two families, the Cohens and the Kellys, live in Hillsboro, a small Midwestern town. They are friends, and there is a romance between young Maurice Cohen (Norman Foster) and Kitty Kelly (June Clyde). When Kitty is offered a screen test by Continental Productions, she takes her whole family to Hollywood. After Kitty becomes a star, the Kellys move into a luxurious mansion. The Cohens arrive in Hollywood to join them, but they are snubbed by the now-wealthy Kellys.

After sound arrives, Kitty's career is ended, and the Kellys are broke again. But Maurice Cohen's songwriting ability enables his family to rise to the top. Now it is their turn to patronize the Kellys. But their luck changes when the cycle of musicals end. Sadder but wiser, the two families return to Hillsboro.

NOTES

Karloff appeared as himself together with other Universal players in the Coconut Grove sequence. This was the sixth in a series of seven *Cohen and Kelly* comedies made by Universal between 1926 and 1933. The characters were created by Aaron Hoffman in his play *Two Blocks Away.*

REVIEW

Still nothing new in thought, gesture, motion or mannerism. . . .

At the Mayfair the mob was . . . unimpressed with the big scene at the Coconut Grove with cut–ins of famous movie stars. Stars were Tom Mix, Lew Ayres, Sidney Fox, Boris Karloff and Genevieve Tobin, all strangely working for Universal.

"Kauf," *Variety*

As Nikko.

The Miracle Man

Paramount   1932.

CREDITS

Directed by Norman Z. McLeod. *Screenplay by* Waldemar Young *and* Samuel Hoffenstein. *Based on a story by* Frank L. Packard *and* Robert H. Davis, *and on the play by* George M. Cohan. *Photography,* David Abel. Released April 1, 1932. Running time: 87 minutes.

CAST

Sylvia Sidney, Chester Morris, Irving Pichel, John Wray, Robert Coogan, Hobart Bosworth, Boris Karloff, Ned Sparks, Lloyd Hughes, Virginia Bruce, Florine McKinney, Frank Darien, Lew Kelly and Jackie Searle.

SYNOPSIS

A trio of big–city crooks led by John Madison (Chester Morris) operate in a Chinese tavern owned by Nikko (Boris Karloff) in return for a percentage. Among the other members of the gang are The Frog (John Wray), a fake cripple, and Helen Smith (Sylvia Sidney), Madison's girl. After Nikko tries to get familiar with Helen, Madison nearly kills the charlatan. Hoping to avoid the police, he hides in a small town and discovers an old faith healer known as The Patriarch (Hobart Bosworth). Madison decides to use him in a racket; Helen will impersonate The Patriarch's long–lost granddaughter and collect money for a fictitious chapel. The Frog will pretend to be cured by the healer.

The scheme works, but the gang sees a genuine cure along with the fake one. Impressed by this, all except Madison reform. As the old healer dies, the gang confess their sins, but they learn he knew all along. Moved, Madison reforms and helps the rest build the chapel.

NOTES

This film was the remake of a 1919 silent, in which Lon Chaney played The Frog. Tyrone Power Sr. was originally supposed to play The Patriarch, but his death prevented this.

REVIEW

It is quite well produced, but the edge is taken off its interest by the familiarity of the story. The dramatic sequence wherein real cripples are cured . . . is, however, just as effective as ever.

The New York Times

With Sylvia Sidney.

Night World

Universal   1932.

CREDITS

Directed by Hobart Henley. *Screenplay by* Richard Schayer. *Based on a story by* P. J. Wolfson *and* Allen Rivkin. *Photography,* Merritt Gerstad. *Editor,* Maurice Pivar. *Dances by* Busby Berkeley. Released May 5, 1932. Running time: 58 minutes.

CAST

Lew Ayres, Mae Clarke, Boris Karloff, Dorothy Revier, Russell Hopton, Bert Roach, Dorothy Peterson, Florence Lake, Gene Morgan, Paisley Noon, Hedda Hopper, Greta Granstedt, Louise Beavers, Sammy Blum, Harry Woods, Eddie Phillips, Tom Tamarez, Clarence Muse, Huntly Gor-

With Mae Clarke, Charles Giblyn and Lew Ayres.

don, George Raft, Robert Emmett O'Connor and Geneva Mitchell.

SYNOPSIS

"Happy" MacDonald (Boris Karloff) is the owner of a night club, and his wife "Mrs. Mac" (Dorothy Revier) works as cashier there. She secretly has an affair with Klauss (Russell Hopton), the dance director of the club's floor show. Ruth Taylor (Mae Clarke) the club's leading dancer, befriends one of the customers, young Michael Rand (Lew Ayres), who tries to blot out the memory of a tragedy by drink. His mother (Hedda Hopper) had surprised his father in the apartment of another woman and killed him. Touched by Ruth's friendship, Michael decides to marry her.

Later that night, a gangster tries to sell Mac-Donald bootleg liquor, but the night club owner refuses. The bootlegger returns with a gunman who murders MacDonald. "Mrs. Mac," who was in league with the gangster, is also murdered. Michael and Ruth accidentally witness her death. Just as the gunman is about to silence them, the police arrive in time and rescue them.

REVIEW

The film is a symphonic arrangement of songs and snatches of human experience. Unfortunately the result is mainly a strained and artificial fiction. The threads have been forced into the pattern, willy–nilly.

Boris Karloff is hampered in his interpretation of the night club owner by his English accent. . . .

Andre D. Sennwald, *The New York Times*

74

With Ernest Thesiger, Eva Moore,
Charles Laughton and Lilian Bond.

The Old Dark House

Universal   1932.

CREDITS

Directed by James Whale. *Produced by* Carl
Laemmle Jr. *Screenplay by* Benn W. Levy. *Based
on the novel by* J. B. Priestley. *Photography,*
Arthur Edeson. *Editor,* Clarence Kolster. *Make-
up,* Jack Pierce. Released October 20, 1932.
Running time: 75 minutes.

CAST

Boris Karloff, Melvyn Douglas, Charles Laughton, Gloria Stuart, Lilian Bond, Ernest Thesiger,
Eva Moore, Raymond Massey, Brember Wills
and John Dudgeon.

SYNOPSIS

Lost in the lonely Welsh mountains, Philip Wav-
erton (Raymond Massey), his wife Margaret
(Gloria Stuart) and Roger Penderel (Melvyn
Douglas) seek refuge from a raging storm at a
nearby ancient house. Its strange occupants are
Horace Femm (Ernest Thesiger), an eccentric
atheist; his sister Rebecca (Eva Moore), a religious fanatic; and Morgan (Boris Karloff), their
mute hulking butler, who becomes homicidally
dangerous when drunk. Two other travelers, Sir
William Porterhouse (Charles Laughton) and
Gladys DuCane (Lilian Bond), a chorus girl, also
receive shelter in the Femm house.

As the storm continues, Morgan gets drunk
and attacks Margaret, but Philip knocks him unconscious. Meanwhile, Penderel and Gladys become attracted to each other and fall in love. In
a remote wing of the old house, Philip and Margaret discover the aged patriarch, Sir Roderick
Femm (John Dudgeon). They learn that his eldest son, Saul (Brember Wills), is a pyromaniac
locked up by Morgan. If set free, he will burn and

With Gloria Stuart.

kill. Insane with hate, Morgan frees Saul who overcomes Penderel and tries to set fire to the house. After a struggle, Penderel kills Saul and the travelers leave the old house, never to return.

NOTES

The Old Dark House marked Karloff's first credited starring role. The film also marked the American film debuts of Charles Laughton and Raymond Massey. In a last–minute casting switch, Russell Hopton was replaced by Melvyn Douglas in the role of Roger Penderel.

REVIEWS

Having discovered through the popularity of . . . *Dracula, Frankenstein* and *Murders in the Rue*

With Brember Wills.

With Melvyn Douglas, Raymond Massey, Charles Laughton and Eva Moore.

77

With actor Russell Hopton on the set.

Morgue that motion picture patrons like to be horrified just as they like to be amused ... Universal Pictures is now offering another shocker in the form of ... J. B. Priestley's *The Old Dark House....*

There is a wealth of talent in this production, and while one may wonder, after witnessing the excited doings, why the motorists ... did not continue on their way immediately after encountering two or three of its occupants, it must be remembered that Mr. Priestley is responsible for their staying, and, as the shadow tale adheres quite closely to the book, he is also responsible for the hysteria that prevails during many of the scenes.

This current thriller, like *Frankenstein*, has the advantage of being directed by James Whale, who again proves his ability. . . .

. . . Mr. Karloff is, of course, thoroughly in his element as Morgan. He leaves no stone unturned to make this character thoroughly disturbing.

Mordaunt Hall, *The New York Times*

This should please the followers of horror melodramas for it has everything to send chills up one's spine—a thunderstorm, a spooky house in a deserted section, candles, half–mad people, and a brutal–looking butler. The individual performances are so excellent that the story is believable. . . . The second half is tensely exciting. The situation showing the madman, at first gentle, and then murderous . . . holds the audience in tense suspense. . . .

Harrison's Reports

Director James Whale (behind Melvyn Douglas) relaxes with cast between scenes.

With Myrna Loy and Charles Starrett.

The Mask of Fu Manchu

Metro–Goldwyn–Mayer   1932.

CREDITS

Directed by Charles Brabin. *Screenplay by* Irene Kuhn, Edgar Allan Woolf *and* John Willard. *Based on the novel by* Sax Rohmer. *Photography,* Tony Gaudio. *Editor,* Ben Lewis. *Makeup,* Cecil Holland. Released November 5, 1932. Running time: 67 minutes.

CAST

Boris Karloff, Lewis Stone, Karen Morley, Charles Starrett, Myrna Loy, Jean Hersholt, Lawrence Grant, David Torrence, Ferdinand Gottschalk, C. Montague Shaw and Willie Fung.

SYNOPSIS

A ruthless oriental Dr. Fu Manchu (Boris Karloff) hopes to possess the ceremonial mask and sword of Genghis Khan. With these sacred relics, Manchu will lead the "teeming hordes of Asia" in exterminating the white race so that he will rule

With Lawrence Grant.

79

the world. Intending to obtain the relics for a British museum, a group of scientists journey to the Gobi Desert to excavate the tomb of Genghis Khan. In order to prevent the relics from falling into the hands of Fu Manchu, Nayland Smith (Lewis Stone) of Scotland Yard accompanies them.

After subjecting members of the expedition to kidnaping, murder and torture, Fu Manchu finally obtains the mask and sword of Genghis Khan. Nayland Smith and Professor Von Berg (Jean Hersholt) are sentenced to death in the crocodile pit and by impalement, while young Terry Granville (Charles Starrett) is fated to be a slave to Fu Manchu's perverted daughter, Fah Lo See (Myrna Loy). But Nayland Smith and Von Berg escape and destroy Fu Manchu with his own

With Lewis Stone (wearing white suit).

With Myrna Loy.

With Myrna Loy, Charles Starrett, Jean Hersholt and Karen Morley.

death ray. The relics are sent to the bottom of the sea to keep them out of the hands of future tyrants.

NOTES

The film encountered the usual production problems familiar to the usual MGM "A" properties. The original director Charles Vidor was replaced with Charles Brabin and much of the scrapped footage was reshot, sometimes for the vaguest reasons. One example: Corpulent Jean Hersholt was substituted for Lewis Stone in the spiked torture device, because some executive reached a conclusion that a fat captive would make the torture sequence more sadistic and hair-raising.

REVIEW

And still the cinema goes busily about its task of terrorizing the children. The latest of the bugaboo symposiums arrived at the Capitol yesterday under the fairly reticent title of *The Mask of Fu Manchu*. Its properties include Boris Karloff, one well-equipped dungeon, several hundred Chinamen, and the proper machinery for persuading a large cast to divulge the location of the mask and sword of the late Genghis Khan. . . .

. . . It is Scotland Yard's intention to frustrate Fu if it takes all winter—and at the Capitol the new film does manage to convey the unhappy impression that it is taking at least that long.

The New York Times

Director Charles Brabin (holding cane) and Karloff (Right) on the set.

82

The Mummy

Universal   1932.

CREDITS

Directed by Karl Freund. *Produced by* Carl Laemmle Jr. *Screenplay by* John L. Balderston. *Based on a story by* Nina Wilcox Putnam *and* Richard Schayer. *Photography,* Charles Stumar. *Editor,* Milton Carruth. *Makeup,* Jack Pierce. Released December 22, 1932. Running time: 72 minutes.

CAST

Boris Karloff, Zita Johann, David Manners, Edward Van Sloan, Arthur Byron, Bramwell Fletcher, Noble Johnson, Leonard Mudie, Katheryn Byron, Eddie Kane, Tony Marlow, James Crane, Henry Victor and Arnold Grey.

SYNOPSIS

In ancient Egypt, Im–Ho–Tep (Boris Karloff), a High Priest, is buried alive after stealing the magic Scroll of Thoth to revive his dead love, an Egyptian princess. The scroll is buried with him. Three thousand seven hundred years later, a British museum unearths the mummy of Im–Ho–Tep and the scroll. After a young archaeologist (Bramwell Fletcher) translates aloud the words of Thoth, the mummy comes to life and mysteriously disappears with the scroll. The young man becomes insane and soon dies. Ten years later, Im–Ho–Tep, disguised as an Egyptian archaeologist, directs another British expedition to the tomb of the princess. After it is transferred to the Cairo Museum, Im–Ho–Tep tries to restore the mummy back to life with the scroll, but discovers that her soul has been reincarnated into the young body of beautiful Helen Grosvenor (Zita Johann).

Dr. Muller (Edward Van Sloan), an authority

With Zita Johann.

With Bramwell Fletcher.

on occult science, discovers Im–Ho–Tep's true identity. Learning Helen is in love with young Frank Whemple (David Manners), he tries to break Im–Ho–Tep's evil spell over her. Despite Muller's precautions, Helen is lured to the museum where Im–Ho–Tep plans to kill her so that they will spend eternal life together. But the statue of Isis comes to life and destroys the scroll and Im–Ho–Tep. Freed of his spell, Helen is finally reunited with Frank.

NOTES

Aside from the modern twentieth–century reincarnation scenes of the Egyptian princess, director Freund also shot footage of her in several phases of the past; ancient Christian, medieval princess, Norse Viking and French nobility. But these added reincarnation scenes were later deleted. Stock footage of Karloff from the ancient Egypt flashbacks in *The Mummy* was effectively matched with Tom Tyler in *The Mummy's Hand* (1940).

With Arthur Byron and
Edward Van Sloan.

"It couldn't be done"—
So Universal did it!

The Mummy
(A KARLOFF Classic)

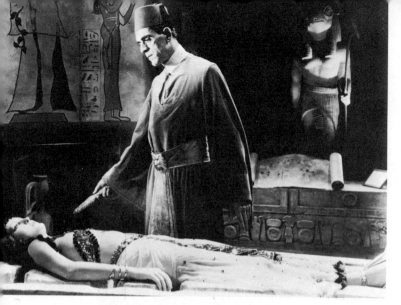

With Zita Johann.

Ironically, stock footage from *The Mummy* and *The Mummy's Hand* turned up briefly in *The Mummy's Curse* (1945).

The impressive statue of Isis in *The Mummy* was later used as the "great god Tao" on the planet Mongo in the serial, *Flash Gordon* (1936).

REVIEWS

Fresh from his amiable massacres in *The Mask of Fu Manchu*, Boris Karloff—now billed austerely as Karloff the Uncanny—is spreading desolation at the Mayfair. That there is a place for a national bogey man in the scheme of things was fulsomely demonstrated by the crowds that clicked past the box office yesterday. In *The Mummy*, Karloff stalks out of his winding cloths after 3700 years of restless sleep, and that is a hideous enough theme to freeze the most callous imagination. . . .

For purposes of terror there are two scenes in *The Mummy* that are weird enough in all conscience. In the first the mummy comes alive. . . . In the second Im–Ho–Tep is embalmed alive, and that moment when the tape is drawn across the man's mouth and nose, leaving only his wild eyes staring out of the coffin, is one of decided horror. But most of *The Mummy* is costume melodrama for the children.

The New York Times

Surely the mantle of the late Lon Chaney will eventually fall upon the actor Karloff, whose portrayal of an unholy thing in this film, aided by magnificent makeup, establishes him as not just a good character actor, but a finished character star.

The Mummy beggars description. It is one of the most unusual talkies ever produced.

Los Angeles Times

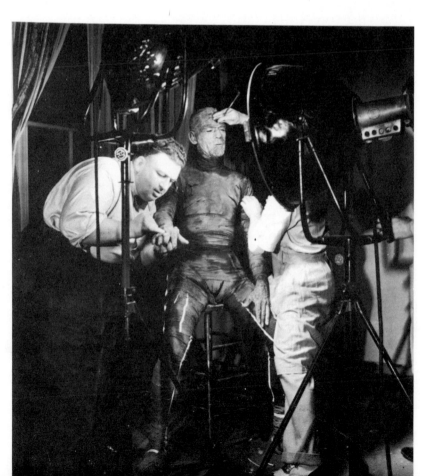

Director Karl Freund assists Jack Pierce (behind lamp) in adjusting Karloff's makeup for the cameras.

The Ghoul

Gaumont-British   1933.

CREDITS

Directed by T. Hayes Hunter. *Screenplay by* Rupert Downing, Roland Pertwee *and* John Hastings Turner. *Based on the novel and play by* Dr. Frank King *and* Leonard J. Hines. *Photography,* Gunther Krampf. *Editor,* Ian Dalrymple. *Make-up,* Heinrich Heitfeld. Released July 1933. Running time: 73 minutes.

CAST

Boris Karloff, Cedric Hardwicke, Ernest Thesiger, Dorothy Hyson, Anthony Bushell, Kathleen Harrison, Harold Huth, D. A. Clarke-Smith, Ralph Richardson and Jack Raine.

SYNOPSIS

A valuable jewel, "The Eternal Light," is stolen from a famous Egyptian tomb and comes into the possession of Professor Morlant (Boris Karloff). Believing in the powers of the ancient Egyptian gods, Morlant is confident it will give him immortality. On his deathbed, the professor instructs his servant, Laing (Ernest Thesiger), to bind the jewel in his hand after his death. Before expiring, he warns Laing if his jewel is stolen, he will rise from the dead to seek revenge.

After Morlant's body is sealed in the tomb behind his house, Laing steals the jewel. The professor's heirs, Betty Harlow (Dorothy Hyson) and

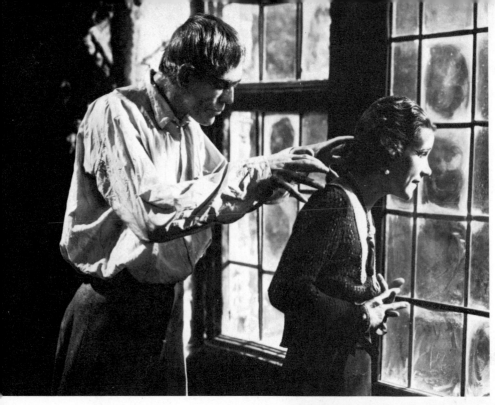

With Kathleen Harrison.

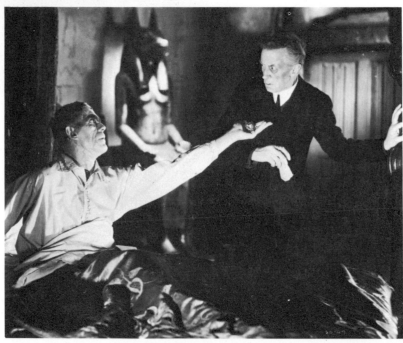

With Ernest Thesiger.

Ralph Morlant (Anthony Bushell), arrive at the ancient house to settle the estate. Obsessed with greed, Morlant's lawyer searches the house for the jewel. He is joined by a bogus parson (Ralph Richardson) and Aga Ben Dragore (Harold Huth) who covet the gem for themselves. After the dead Morlant discovers his jewel stolen, he grimly rises from his tomb to retrieve it. The professor strangles his servant and regains his jewel.

He returns to his tomb and dies finally. The police arrest the lawyer, parson and Dragore after they attempt to steal the jewel. "The Eternal Light" is returned to the heirs who use it to start a new life.

NOTES

Karloff's first British–produced film was also England's first major effort to capitalize on the large horror cycle. To insure its success, Gaumont–

British imported one of UFA's top makeup men to create Karloff's makeup. In 1962, *The Ghoul* was remade in England as a knockabout comedy called *No Place Like Homicide!* Its cast included some of the *Carry On* gang with Philip O'Flynn recreating Karloff's original role.

REVIEW

. . . Too scattered a story and characterization to work up any kind of exciting climax, and it seems too slow. . . .

Mr. Karloff is again a menacing brute to see. His feats of makeup are effective . . . he does resemble, even before his demise, something dead rather than alive . . . he gives a curiously supernatural impression always by the blankness in the eyes, and by that strange robot gait of his which seems to be directed by a mind outside himself.

New York Herald Tribune

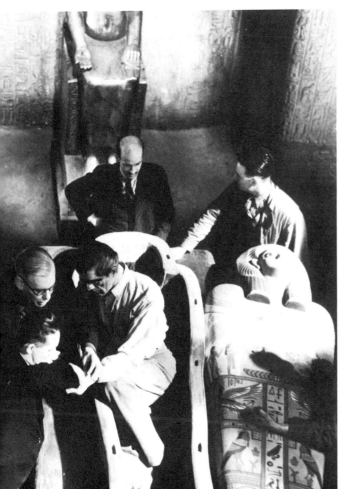

With Director T. Hayes Hunter
(wearing glasses) on the set.

89

With J. M. Kerrigan, Paul Hanson, Victor McLaglen, Alan Hale, Brandon Hurst, Reginald Denny, Billy Bevan and Douglas Walton.

The Lost Patrol

RKO Radio   1934.

CREDITS

Directed by John Ford. *Screenplay by* Dudley Nichols *and* Garrett Fort. *Based on the story* Patrol *by* Philip MacDonald. *Photography,* Harold Wenstrom. *Editor,* Paul Weatherwax. *Musical score,* Max Steiner. Released February 16, 1934. Running time: 75 minutes.

CAST

Victor McLaglen, Boris Karloff, Wallace Ford, Reginald Denny, J. M. Kerrigan, Billy Bevan, Alan Hale, Brandon Hurst, Douglas Walton, Sammy Stein, Howard Wilson, Paul Hanson and Neville Clark.

SYNOPSIS

During the First World War, a patrol of British cavalrymen find themselves stranded in the Mesopotamian Desert. Only one officer in the group had knowledge of their location, their destination and their orders. But he was killed by an Arab sniper. The veteran sergeant (Victor McLaglen) takes command. After they camp at an oasis, Arabs kill one sentry and steal their horses. The soldiers find themselves surrounded by unseen enemies. One by one, they are picked off by snipers. After two soldiers try to go for help, their bodies are returned, murdered. Only three remain: Morelli (Wallace Ford), the sergeant and Sanders (Boris Karloff), a religious fanatic.

A plane flies over to rescue them, but the pilot is killed after he lands. Gone insane, Sanders fashions a makeshift cross and starts across the desert. Morelli rushes after him, but both are shot. Alone, the sergeant holds off the attacking Arabs

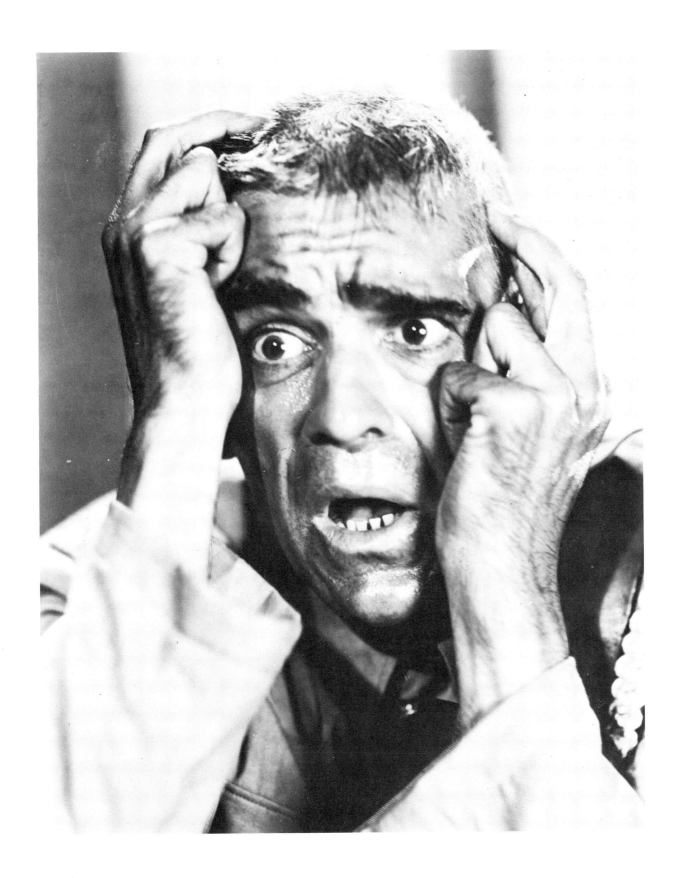

with a machine gun until a rescue party arrives.

NOTES

The film was shot entirely on location near Yuma, Arizona, where the temperature sometimes went over 110 degrees. Max Steiner's score was the first for a dramatic picture to be nominated for an Oscar. *The Lost Patrol* was a remake of an earlier English film version (1929) of the novel.

REVIEW

Not a woman in the cast and substantially little as to story, but under the weight of suspense, dialogue and competency of direction, *Lost Patrol* tips the scales favorably as entertainment . . .

. . . As a Bible nut, Boris Karloff is on a somewhat different assignment. He gives a fine account of himself.

"Char," *Variety*

Rehearsing with Director John Ford (pointing) on location.

The House of Rothschild

United Artists   1934.

CREDITS

Directed by Alfred Werker. *Screenplay by* Nunnally Johnson. *Based on the play by* George Hembert Westley. *Photography,* Peverell Marley. *Editors,* Alan McNeil *and* Barbara McLean. Released April 6, 1934. Running time: 86 minutes.

CAST

George Arliss, Boris Karloff, Loretta Young, Robert Young, C. Aubrey Smith, Arthur Byron, Helen Westley, Reginald Owen, Florence Arliss, Alan Mowbray, Holmes Herbert, Paul Harvey, Ivan Simpson, Noel Madison, Murray Kinnell and George Renavent.

SYNOPSIS

During the late 1700s in a German ghetto, moneylender Mayer Rothschild (George Arliss) instructs his sons to create banking houses in the five capital cities of Europe. Under the leadership of Nathan (George Arliss), the Rothschilds rise from obscurity to become the foremost banking house in Europe. During the Napoleonic Wars, the Rothschilds secretly lend financial aid to Austria, Italy, Prussia and England to crush Napoleon. Following Napoleon's defeat, Rothschild attempts to lend money to the allies to restore economic security to France. But the anti–Semitic Prussian ambassador, Baron Ledrantz (Boris Karloff), blocks Nathan's bid because he is a Jew. Learning that Nathan has raided the bond market in retaliation, Ledrantz incites bloody pogroms in the Jewish ghettos.

But Nathan's moment finally arrives. Learning of Napoleon's escape and preparation for war, Ledrantz and the other ministers are forced to plead for aid from Rothschild to defeat Napoleon. In return, the anti–Semitic pogroms are ceased for good. After Wellington defeats Napoleon at Waterloo, Nathan is made a baron by the King of England.

NOTES

The House of Rothschild was the most lavish film produced by Darryl F. Zanuck and Joseph Schenck for their new company, 20th–Century Productions (which soon evolved into 20th Century-Fox). Aside from being one of the year–old company's biggest hits, the anti–Semitic outbursts in the film unintentionally focused critical attention upon the current Nazi Jew–baitings in Germany.

The brief closing sequence showing Rothschild being publicly honored was photographed in the early Technicolor three–color process.

With George Arliss.

REVIEW

In the person of Nathan Rothschild, overlord of the international banking house that shaped the destiny of Europe . . . George Arliss has found his most congenial role since *Disraeli*.

The story provides a fascinating study of international intrigue in the nineteenth century. It is presented straight–forwardly, without apology or sentimentality.

Because of its lack of dramatic sequence, the picture lapses into . . . passages that become monotonous. The injection of a romantic episode between Nathan's daughter and a Gentile British officer, with its . . . mixed–marriage problem, is tritely handled.

On the whole, the picture has been skillfully cast . . . there are good performances by Reginald Owen and Boris Karloff.

New York Evening Post

With George Arliss (second from Left), Arthur Byron, Alan Mowbray and George Renavent.

With Bela Lugosi.

The Black Cat

Universal   1934.

CREDITS

Directed by Edgar Ulmer. *Produced by* Carl
Laemmle Jr. *Screenplay by* Peter Ruric. *Based
on the story by* Edgar Allan Poe. *Photography,*
John Mescall. *Editor,* Ray Curtiss. *Musical score,*
Heinz Roemheld. Released May 7, 1934. Run-
ning time: 65 minutes.

CAST

Boris Karloff, Bela Lugosi, David Manners, Jac-
queline Wells, Lucille Lund, Harry Cording,
Egon Brecher, Anna Duncan, Henry Armetta,
Albert Conti, Tony Marlo, Paul Weigel, George
Davis, Herman Bing, Luis Alberni, Michael
Mark, King Baggott, Paul Panzer and John Car-
radine.

SYNOPSIS

Newlyweds Peter (David Manners) and Joan
Alison (Jacqueline Wells) are traveling to a European resort. They are joined by Dr. Vitus Verdegast (Bela Lugosi), on his way to visit a former
Army engineer, Hjalmar Poelzig (Boris Karloff).
Traveling by car, their vehicle crashes in the desolate Hungarian countryside. The travelers obtain
shelter in Poelzig's house, constructed over the
site of a mined military fort. Verdegast accuses
the architect of causing a military defeat costing
him fifteen years in prison and the lives of ten
thousand men. He also demands the whereabouts
of his wife and daughter, abducted by Poelzig. In
a subterranean chamber, Verdegast discovers the
dead body of his wife, preserved in a glass case.

With Bela Lugosi.

With Bela Lugosi

Refusing to believe his wife and daughter died of natural causes, he attempts to shoot Poelzig. But the appearance of a black cat completely unnerves him. Soon, the newlyweds learn they are Poelzig's prisoners. Verdegast plays a game of chess for Joan's freedom, but loses.

Poelzig, leader of a cult of devil-worshippers, casts Joan as a sacrificial victim in a Black Mass. But Verdegast and his servant, Thamal (Harry Cording), rescue her from the ceremonial altar. To his horror, Verdegast discovers the dead body of his daughter, a victim of Poelzig's maniacal rages. Filled with revenge, he binds his enemy to a rack and skins him alive. Believing Verdegast about to harm Joan also, Peter shoots him. Mortally wounded, Verdegast blows up the entire house after permitting the young couple to escape.

With Jacqueline Wells, Paul Panzer and Michael Mark.

With Lucille Lund and Bela Lugosi.

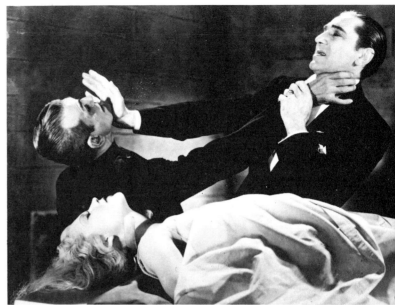

With Lucille Lund and Bela Lugosi.

REVIEW

Universal has of course proceeded on the theory that if *Frankenstein* was a monster and *Dracula* a nightmare, the two in combination would constitute the final cast in cinematic delirium . . . with the aid of heavily shadowed lighting and mausoleum–like architecture, a certain eerieness has been achieved.

. . . Skinning alive is not new. It was done in a Gouverneur Morris story, *The Man Behind the Door,* filmed during the war. A truly horrible and nauseating bit of extreme sadism, its inclusion in a motion picture is dubious showmanship.

Karloff and Lugosi are sufficiently sinister and convincingly demented. Jacqueline Wells spends most of her footage in swoons.

Variety

Between scenes with Anna Duncan, Director Edgar Ulmer and David Manners.

The Gift of Gab

Universal   1934.

CREDITS

Directed by Karl Freund. *Screenplay by* Rian James *and* Lou Breslow. *Based on a story by* Jerry Wald *and* Philip G. Epstein. *Photography,* George Robinson *and* Harold Wenstrom. *Editor,* Raymond Curtis. Released September 24, 1934. Running time: 71 minutes.

CAST

Edmund Lowe, Gloria Stuart, Ruth Etting, Phil Baker, Ethel Waters, Alice White, Alexander Woollcott, Victor Moore, Hugh O'Connell, Helen Vinson, Gene Austin, Tom Hanlon, Henry Armetta, Andy Devine, Wini Shaw, Sterling Holloway, Sid Walker, Skins Miller, Jack Harling, Edwin Maxwell, James Flavin, Billy Barty, Paul Lukas, Douglass Montgomery, Graham McNamee, The Downey Sisters, Douglas Fowley, Chester Morris, Roger Pryor, Boris Karloff, Bela

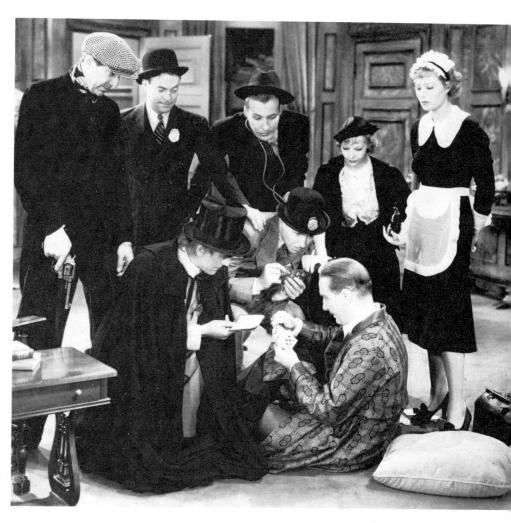

With Bela Lugosi, Chester Morris, Douglass Montgomery, Roger Pryor, Paul Lukas, June Knight and Binnie Barnes.

Lugosi, Binnie Barnes, June Knight and Sidney Skolsky.

SYNOPSIS

Philip Gabney (Edmund Lowe), a smooth-talking radio announcer, is hired to revive interest in a failing radio show. His ideas soon make him the sensation of the airwaves. After hiring a press agent, he begins to believe his own publicity and becomes an egocentric. During one of his late drinking parties, Gabney forgets to broadcast the arrival of a British flier crossing the ocean. Instead, he fakes an interview in his studio. Gabney is fired for this deception and becomes a drunk.

With the assistance of Barbara Kelton (Gloria Stuart), head of the program department, Gabney is given another chance. The announcer risks his life in giving his audience the first parachute broadcast description of a plane wreck. He is re-stored to national popularity and marries Barbara on the air.

NOTES

Karloff played the "Phantom" and Lugosi a French apache dancer together with a half-dozen stars who appeared in a burlesque murder-mystery conceived by Gabney at the beginning of the film. Though the sketch was technically a broadcast, it was photographed in the usual atmospheric style necessary to produce the required chills.

REVIEW

The total effect . . . is that of an endless and progressively soporific procession of one-reelers strung together to make a full-length feature, and it constitutes a minor miracle that the sum of so much talent should be such meager entertainment.

The New York Times

With Anne Darling.

The Bride of Frankenstein

Universal   1935.

CREDITS

Directed by James Whale. *Produced by* Carl Laemmle Jr. *Screenplay by* William Hurlbut *and* John L. Balderston. *Based on the novel by* Mary Wollstonecraft Shelley. *Photography,* John Mescall. *Editor,* Ted Kent. *Musical score,* Franz Waxman. *Makeup,* Jack Pierce. Released May 6, 1935. Running time: 75 minutes.

CAST

Boris Karloff, Colin Clive, Valerie Hobson, Elsa Lanchester, Ernest Thesiger, O. P. Heggie, Dwight Frye, E. E. Clive, Una O'Connor, Anne Darling, Douglas Walton, Gavin Gordon, Neil Fitzgerald, Reginald Barlow, Mary Gordon, Ted Billings, Lucien Prival, John Carradine, Maurice Black, Billy Barty, Norman Ainsley, Joan Woodbury, Arthur S. Byron, Josephine McKim, Kansas De-Forrest, Peter Shaw, Walter Brennan and Helen Parrish.

SYNOPSIS

Authoress Mary Shelley (Elsa Lanchester) is persuaded by Lord Byron (Gavin Gordon) to continue her story of Frankenstein's creation (Boris Karloff) following his presumed demise in a burning mill. After the parents of the drowned girl discover the Monster had escaped the fire, they fall into his clutches and are murdered. Seek-

With E. E. Clive (Left).

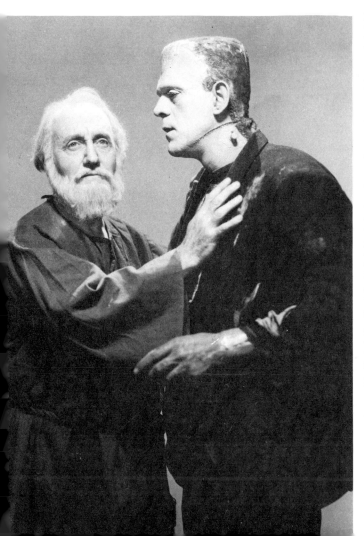

With O. P. Heggie.

ing companionship, the creature rescues a shepherdess from drowning, but he is captured by the villagers. Escaping from the village jail, he terrorizes the countryside, killing several persons. The Monster is befriended by a blind hermit (O. P. Heggie) who teaches him to speak. But two hunters arrive and reveal the identity of the creature.

While recuperating from his near-fatal encounter with his creation, Henry Frankenstein (Colin Clive) is visited by his former teacher, Dr. Pretorious (Ernest Thesiger). Pretorious reveals to Henry his experiments in the creation of life: tiny human beings in glass jars. Eager to create a mate for the Monster, Pretorious persuades Henry to help him by abducting his bride, Elizabeth (Valerie Hobson). After Pretorious' servant, Karl (Dwight Frye), murders a young woman to secure a human heart, the scientists' creation comes to life during a violent electrical storm. But when the moment arrives for the Monster to claim his Mate (Elsa Lanchester), she recoils from him and shrieks in terror. Griefstricken, the

101

Monster destroys himself and everyone else after permitting Frankenstein to join Elizabeth in safety.

NOTES

During the writing of the *Bride* screenplay, the writers considered having Frankenstein's wife murdered, so that her brain would be inserted into the skull of the Monster's bride, but this idea was abandoned. Also, Claude Rains was originally slated for the role of Pretorious, but other commitments made this impossible and Ernest Thesiger was finally chosen.

Karloff injured his left side during the shooting of the flooded cellar scene and received special infrared ray treatments throughout the rest of the filming.

The final release differed from the longer preview version as over fifteen minutes of footage was cut. The prologue containing references to the scandalous behavior of the three writers (Lord Byron, Percy and Mary Shelley) and its deletion made the remaining dialogue at times curiously uneven. One lengthy sequence was removed: a coroner's investigation is interrupted by the sudden arrival of the Monster, who pulls the Burgomaster through a window and thrashes him about; this inspires Karl Glutz, the village idiot, to kill his miserly uncle, rob his hoarded savings and place the blame on the Monster. To fill in this missing continuity gap, a short sequence was shot and inserted at the last moment in which the Monster encounters a gypsy tribe. This is one sequence in the film that has no musical score. Other cuts include Pretorious' embittered speech accusing Frankenstein of bungling Pretorious' theories of creating life and letting him take the blame for them; some dialogue exchanges between Pretorious and Karl; the escaping Monster crushing a villager, and so forth.

The original ending had Henry and Elizabeth perish in the lab explosion. A new happy ending was substituted instead whereby they escape in the nick of time. However, one scene remains in which alert viewers can spot Henry being buried in the lab under falling debris.

Stock footage from *Bride* later turned up briefly in flashback sequences in *Ghost of Frankenstein* (1942) and *House of Dracula* (1945).

Franz Waxman's score for *Bride* was so successful that Universal reused sections of it in later films, notably the *Flash Gordon, Buck Rogers* serials and a few "B" features.

REVIEWS

William Hurlbut and John L. Balderston, who contrived this follow-up film evidence a lot of ingenuity by making quite plausible the return of the Monster.

Karloff . . . is, of course, at top form as the

With Elsa Lanchester.

Monster using the same bizarre makeup as in the first . . . film. He nevertheless manages to invest the character with some subtleties of emotion that are surprisingly real and touching. Especially . . . where he meets a blind man who, not knowing that he's talking to a Monster, makes a friend of him.

John Mescall at the camera managed to create a large number of unusual angles and process shots which help the film tremendously. It is this excellent camerawork coupled with an eerie but lingering musical score by Franz Waxman (one of Hitler's gifts to Hollywood) that gives a great deal of the film its real horror. . . .

"Kauf," *Variety*

. . . The "big moment" when the synthetic woman begins to breathe is duly spellbinding. For those

With Colin Clive and Ernest Thesiger.

On the set with Director James Whale and Cameraman John Mescall.

who got a thrill out of *Frankenstein* . . . Karloff has new thrills waiting. The Monster has learned to speak.

Miss Lanchester, though her part is . . . small, manages to make the Mate worthy of Karloff's gruesome Monster, and she is indeed a strange–looking "new woman" with hair that stands out a foot from her head and movements as staccato as modern music.

New York Herald Tribune

Karloff comes again to terrify the children, frighten the women and play a jiggling tune upon masculine spines . . .

. . . Karloff's makeup should not be permitted to pass from the screen. The Monster should become an institution, like Charlie Chan . . . James Whale, who directed the earlier picture, has done another excellent job; the settings, photography and makeup . . . contribute their important elements to a first–rate horror film.

The New York Times

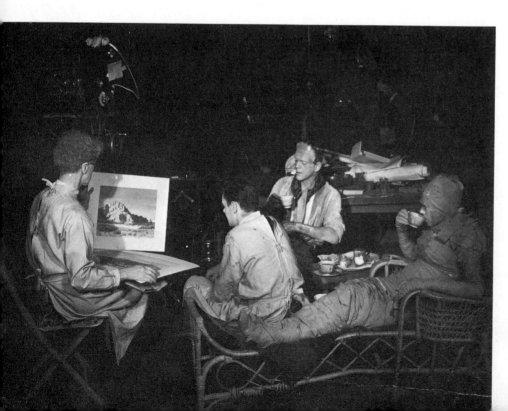

Relaxing between scenes with Ernest Thesiger, Colin Clive and Elsa Lanchester.

With Katherine DeMille and
Marian Marsh.

The Black Room

Columbia   1935.

CREDITS

Directed by Roy William Neill. *Screenplay by*
Henry Meyers *and* Arthur Strawn. *Photography,*
Al Seigler. *Editor,* Richard Cahoon. Released
July 15, 1935. Running time: 68 minutes.

CAST

Boris Karloff, Marian Marsh, Robert Allen, Thurston Hall, Katherine DeMille, John Buckler,
Henry Kolker, Colin Tapley, Torben Meyer,
Egon Brecher, Jon Bleifer, Fredrik Vogeding,
Edward Van Sloan, Lois Lindsay and Herbert
Evans.

With Thurston Hall and John Buckler.

With Katherine DeMille.

106

With Torben Meyer, Joseph Singer, George Burr McGannon, Jon Bleifer and Henry Rowland.

SYNOPSIS

In the early 1800s, there is great dismay when twins are born to a ruler in a Czechoslovakian province. A legend persists that the arrival of twins means the De Berghman family will perish when the younger twin will slay the elder in the Black Room. As the years pass, Gregor (Boris Karloff), the eldest, acquires a reputation for brutality and sadism. The peasants become fearful as their women mysteriously disappear in the baron's castle. When an angry mob confronts the baron with their accusations, Gregor abdicates in favor of his kind-hearted brother, Anton (Boris Karloff), recently returned home. Then Gregor secretly murders Anton in the Black Room and impersonates him.

With Marian Marsh.

107

Director Roy William Neill (holding dog) and cast relax between scenes.

Soon Gregor obtains permission to marry the beautiful Thea (Marian Marsh), daughter of Col. Hassel (Thurston Hall). But her father discovers his identity and is murdered. Before the marriage ceremony is completed, Anton's dog betrays Gregor's true identity. Shocked at this deception, the peasants pursue the baron back to the castle. Hiding in the Black Room, Gregor is discovered by Anton's dog and knocked into a pit. He is impaled by a knife clutched by the dead Anton. The family prophecy is fulfilled with the death of the last of the De Berghmans.

REVIEWS

. . . Everything eerie has been injected into the picture . . . Roy William Neill has directed as well as possible a . . . obvious story . . . kudos . . . must go to Al Seigler for his beautiful camera work and to the makeup man . . . The double exposures of Karloff in dual character are exceptionally fine and Neill has handled these episodes with finesse. As for Karloff, he is his usual self, in practically every sequence . . .

Variety

. . . Karloff differentiates well between the twin brothers, and gives a sound performance.

Ingenious "horror" plot . . .

Kine Weekly

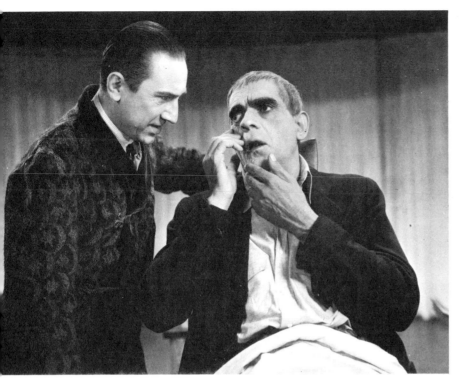

With Bela Lugosi.

The Raven

Universal   1935.

CREDITS

Directed by Louis Friedlander. *Screenplay by* David Boehm. *Based on the poem by* Edgar Allan Poe. *Photography,* Charles Stumar. *Editor,* Alfred Akst. *Ballet sequence by* Theodore Kosloff. *Make-up,* Jack Pierce. Released July 22, 1935. Running time: 61 minutes.

CAST

Boris Karloff, Bela Lugosi, Irene Ware, Lester Matthews, Samuel Hinds, Inez Courtney, Ian Wolfe, Spencer Charters, Maidel Turner, Arthur Hoyt and Walter Miller.

SYNOPSIS

Obsessed by the works of Edgar Allan Poe, Dr. Vollin (Bela Lugosi) constructs a dungeon in his

With Bela Lugosi.

With Samuel Hinds.

basement containing Poe–like torture devices. After the surgeon saves the life of Jean Thatcher (Irene Ware), he falls desperately in love with her. Her father, Judge Thatcher (Samuel Hinds), tries to stop this because she is engaged to Dr. Jerry Halden (Lester Matthews). Driven to the edge of insanity, Vollin determines to revenge himself against Jean and the others who defied him. Bateman (Boris Karloff), a notorious criminal, visits Dr. Vollin and begs him to change his features in order to escape the law. Vollin agrees to do so. But the operation leaves Bateman a horribly mutilated monster. In return for restoring his features back to normal, Bateman agrees to aid Vollin in his plans for revenge.

After Jean, her father and young Halden arrive at Vollin's home for a houseparty, Bateman abducts Judge Thatcher and manacles him below a slowly descending blade in the cellar. Jean and Jerry also fall into Vollin's clutches. He imprisons

With Bela Lugosi and Samuel Hinds.

110

With Bela Lugosi, Irene Ware and Lester Matthews.

Lugosi removes bandages from Karloff's face, which he had disfigured horribly . . .

Harrison's Reports

A good horror flicker . . . suggested by the Poe classic . . . Boehm's adaptation wanders not a little . . . Director Friedlander . . . has kept the pace at a nice pitch, stripping it down to its fundamentals and letting the shock troupers, Karloff and Lugosi, do their worst . . .

. . . Maintains Universal high batting average with the shockers, only this one looks the least costly of 'em—without any obvious cheating . . .

"Abel," *Variety*

them in a room to be crushed to death. Bateman protests Jean's horrible death and frees them. Mortally wounded by Vollin, Bateman drags the madman into the chamber. After Thatcher is rescued from the deadly pendulum, Vollin dies in the torture device he constructed for his victims.

REVIEWS

Followers of horror melodrama will get a full evening's entertainment out of *The Raven* . . . it has some hair-raising situations . . . All that has been left of the famous . . . Poe poem is the title. A statuette of a raven, which Lugosi kept on his desk . . . was the excuse for the use of the title . . . A situation that will give shudders is . . . when

With Ian Wolfe, Inez Courtney, Lester Matthews, Irene Ware and Bela Lugosi.

Director Louis Friedlander (leaning on table) and cast on the set.

The Invisible Ray

Universal   1936.

CREDITS

Directed by Lambert Hillyer. *Screenplay by* John Colton. *Based on a story by* Howard Higgin *and* Douglas Hodges. *Photography,* George Robinson. *Editor,* Bernard Barton. *Musical score,* Franz Waxman. Released January 20, 1936. Running time: 79 minutes.

CAST

Boris Karloff, Bela Lugosi, Frances Drake, Frank Lawton, Walter Kingsford, Beulah Bondi, Violet Kemble Cooper, Nydia Westman, Daniel Haines, George Renavent, Paul Weigel, Adele St. Maur, Frank Reicher, Lawrence Stewart, Inez Seabury, Ernie Adams and Walter Miller.

SYNOPSIS

With a specially created telescope, Dr. Janos Rukh (Boris Karloff) successfully proves that ages ago a meteorite landed in Africa containing an unknown, but super-powerful element. Dr. Benet (Bela Lugosi) agrees to form an expedition led by Rukh to locate the element. Proceeding alone into the Mountains of the Moon, Rukh discovers "Radium X," a substance more powerful than radium. But he becomes contaminated by the radioactive element and learns that his touch means death. To counteract the radioactive luminosity and its horrible results, Dr. Benet creates a temporary antidote from a sample.

Believing that Benet and the others have stolen his discovery by presenting it to the Scientific Congress, Rukh is consumed with revenge. His brain affected by the radioactivity, he murders several members of the expedition, including

With Snowflake.

Dr. Benet. After Rukh nearly murders his wife (Frances Drake), his mother (Violet Kemble Cooper) destroys his antidote. Becoming consumed with the poisons of Radium X, Rukh becomes a ball of fire as he leaps from a window to his death.

NOTES

The film introduced Karloff to the role which he would repeat throughout his career: a sympathetic scientist whose remarkable discovery somehow makes him a threat to society. Though certainly not the first science-fiction film, *The Invisible Ray* was the first modern effort whose theme and plot motivations fixed the pattern for dozens of science-fiction films of the post–World War II era. Universal intended to make another follow-up with Karloff and Lugosi in a similar theme. But

With Beulah Bondi, Walter Kingsford, Bela Lugosi, Frances Drake and Frank Lawton.

With Bela Lugosi.

instead of a deadly radioactive man, this time Karloff would be an electrical monstrosity. A script was fashioned titled, *The Man in the Cab,* but the production was abandoned as public interest waned in horror and science–fiction films late that year. It was later filmed in late 1940 under a new title, *Man Made Monster,* with Lionel Atwill and Lon Chaney Jr. in the Lugosi–Karloff roles respectively.

The Invisible Ray's director, Lambert Hillyer, was a specialist in westerns and made only one other horror film: *Dracula's Daughter* (released later that same year). Hillyer cleverly utilized a few standing sets from *Flash Gordon* (also being filmed at the same time) and inserted stock footage of electrical machines from *Frankenstein.* Ironically, stock footage from *The Invisible Ray* was used later in a Lugosi serial, *The Phantom Creeps* (1939).

John P. Fulton's special effects contributed a

With Bela Lugosi.

114

With Violet Kemble Cooper.

large part to the success of *The Invisible Ray*. His reproduction of the battle of the suns and stars in the nebula Andromeda as it occurred millions of years ago was considered by many to be an innovation for its time. To insure box-office success for the film, Universal deliberately cloaked its methods for producing the effects in secrecy during the filming.

REVIEW

It isn't blood-curdling to the point achieved in some Hollywoodian efforts, but it is different and fairly entertaining . . .

. . . [Karloff] and Lugosi stand away out in an otherwise average cast.

"Char," *Variety*

With Director Lambert Hillyer and Cameraman George Robinson on the set.

115

With Addison Richards (Center).

The Walking Dead

Warner Bros.   1936.

CREDITS

Directed by Michael Curtiz. *Screenplay by* Ewart Adamson, Peter Milne, Robert Andrews *and* Lilli Hayward. *Photography,* Hal Mohr. *Editor,* Tommy Pratt. *Makeup,* Perc Westmore. Released March 14, 1936. Running time: 65 minutes.

CAST

Boris Karloff, Ricardo Cortez, Edmund Gwenn, Marguerite Churchill, Warren Hull, Barton Mac-Lane, Henry O'Neill, Joseph King, Paul Harvey, Robert Strange, Joseph Sawyer, Eddie Acuff, Ruth Robinson, Addison Richards, Kenneth Harlan, Miki Morita, Adrian Rosley, Milt Kibbee and Bill Elliot.

SYNOPSIS

A group of big–city racketeers led by Nolan (Ricardo Cortez) arrange to have an honest judge bumped off. To free themselves from suspicion, they frame an ex–con, John Ellman (Boris Karloff), for the murder. To make sure that Ellman will not escape conviction, Nolan acts as his attorney. Just before Ellman is executed for the crime, two young eyewitnesses to the crime try to inform his attorney of Ellman's innocence. But Nolan deliberately delays communicating this information until it is too late. Ellman is executed in the electric chair.

Dr. Beaumont (Edmund Gwenn), a scientist noted for restoring life to dead animals, requests permission to try to revive the electrocuted man. During a spectacular operation utilizing the latest scientific equipment, Dr. Beaumont restores Ellman to life. Acting as if controlled by a higher

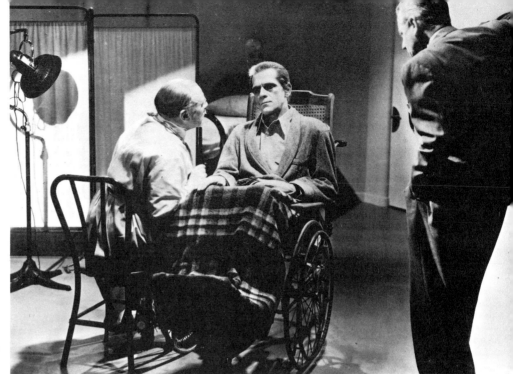

With Edmund Gwenn and Henry O'Neill.

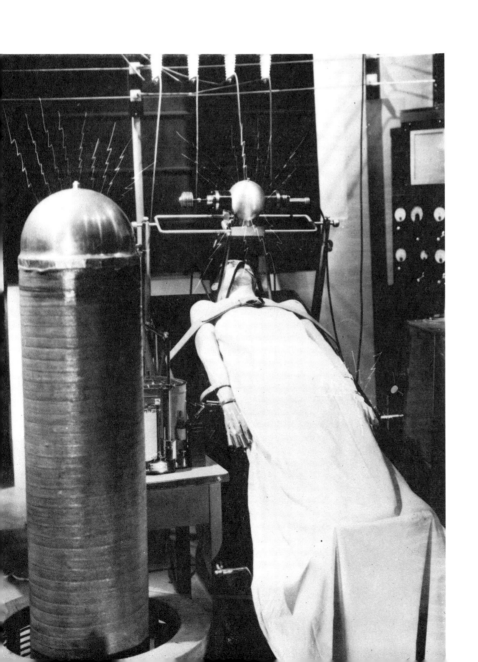

power, Ellman visits each of the racketeers and frightens them into a violent death. The remaining ringleaders track down Ellman in a deserted cemetery on a rainy night and shoot him. Ironically, they are electrocuted in their getaway car when it crashes into a pole carrying high–tension wires. Ellman admonishes Beaumont to leave the dead to themselves and dies once more.

REVIEWS

Karloff . . . is less macabre here than in his *Frankenstein* roles, but is still sufficiently weird to remain in keeping with former characterizations.

The production values are excellent, especially those laboratory scenes during which the dead man is brought back to life . . .

Motion Picture Herald

The Walking Dead is rather more successful than the run of horror dramas . . . horror element is minimized . . . instead of invoking the supernatural, depends for its terror upon the idea of a living corpse, homesick for the graveyard, walking lonely and unhappy through a world of bewildering humans. It's gruesome . . . in its own way . . .

. . . The last reels are melodramatic but repetitious—the . . . imagination seems to have run out. Mr. Karloff, as the kindly, gentle semighost, is at his best . . .

New York *Sun*

With Barton MacLane and Ricardo Cortez.

On the set with Edmund Gwenn, visitor H. G. Wells and Jack Warner.

With Frank Cellier.

The Man Who Lived Again

Gaumont–British   1936.

CREDITS

Directed by Robert Stevenson. *Screenplay by* L. DuGarde Peach, Sidney Gilliat *and* John L. Balderston. *Photography,* Jack Cox. *Editors,* R. E. Dearing *and* Alfred Roome. Released September 11, 1936. Running time: 66 minutes.

CAST

Boris Karloff, Anna Lee, John Loder, Frank Cellier, Donald Calthrop, Cecil Parker and Lynn Harding.

SYNOPSIS

In a lonely manor on the outskirts of London, Dr. Laurience (Boris Karloff) creates a strange apparatus capable of transposing the mind of one person to the body of another. His only companion is Clayton (Donald Calthrop), a paralytic with a fatal brain disease, mysteriously kept alive by the scientist. Impressed, Lord Haslewood (Frank Cellier), a powerful publisher, finances Laurience's experiments at his Institute in London. After the scientist explains his theory to the Medical Society following a publicity buildup, he is laughed off the platform. Believing Laurience a charlatan, Haslewood withdraws his support. Enraged, Laurience traps the publisher in his machine and exchanges the brain of the crippled Clayton with Haslewood's. Both men soon die.

Half-mad, Laurience intends to share his secret of eternal youth with his beautiful assistant, Clare (Anna Lee); they could live forever by transferring their minds through the years to younger bodies. Learning she plans to marry young Dick Haslewood (John Loder), he plans to eliminate his rival and win Clare's affections. After committing a murder, Laurience exchanges his mind with Haslewood's so he will be executed for the murder he committed. But this deception fails and Laurience is mortally wounded while escaping from the police. Clare retransfers their minds

119

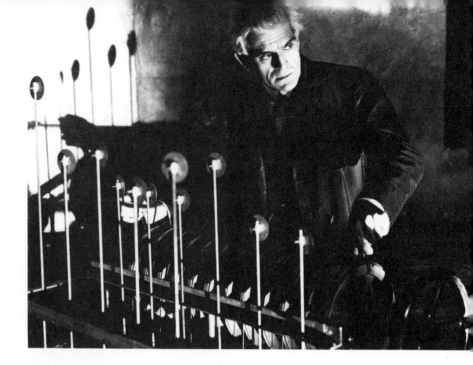

back into their original bodies in the nick of time. After Clare promises to destroy his invention, Dr. Laurience dies, taking his secrets with him.

REVIEW

. . . Produced in England . . . settings are on the grand scale and the players perform as melodramatically as any California director could have demanded.

Karloff . . . is a matchlessly amusing monster. It is entertaining to see him resume the role.

Bland Johaneson, New York *Daily Mirror*

With Anna Lee.

With Donald Calthrop.

With Mona Goya.

Juggernaut

Grand National   1936.

CREDITS

Directed by Henry Edwards. *Screenplay by* Cyril Campion, H. Fowler Mear *and* H. Fraenkel. *Based on a story by* Alice Campbell. *Photography,* Sidney Blythe. *Editor,* Michael Chorlton. Released September 18, 1936. Running time: 64 minutes.

CAST

Boris Karloff, Joan Wyndham, Arthur Margetson, Mona Goya, Anthony Ireland, Morton Selten, Nina Boucicault, Gibb McLaughlin, J. H. Roberts and V. Rietti.

SYNOPSIS

Due to lack of funds, Dr. Sartorius (Boris Karloff) is forced to give up his expériments for a paralysis cure. He is visited by Lady Yvonne Clifford (Mona Goya), extravagant wife of ailing cotton millionaire, elderly Sir Charles Clifford (Morton Selten). Lady Clifford requests Sartorius's aid to gain control of her husband's wealth. Determined to stop at nothing to obtain funds to complete his scientific research, the fanatical doctor agrees to poison her husband and make it appear he died of natural causes for her promise of 20,000 pounds.

After Dr. Sartorius is established as the Clifford mansion physician, Sir Charles grows noticeably weaker. Suspecting foul play, he transfers the control of his wealth to Roger (Arthur Marget-

With Mona Goya, Joan Wyndham and Morton Selten (on bed).

son), his son by an earlier marriage. After discovering the new financial arrangements, Sartorius is instructed to give his patient another "injection." That night Sir Clifford dies. The doctor and Yvonne plan to kill young Roger in the same manner, but the doctor's nurse (Joan Wyndham) accuses him of murder. Realizing he is trapped, Sartorius plunges the deadly needle in his own arm instead. As he expires, Lady Clifford is arrested after her part in the murder plot is exposed.

REVIEW

. . . Karloff, minus his . . . weird makeup, but still as sinister as ever, is an evil French doctor . . . in the feeble, fumbling English melodrama called *Juggernaut* . . .

. . . the film has little about it to recommend unless it is its courage in braving the competition that now exists along Broadway.

William Boehnel, *New York World-Telegram*

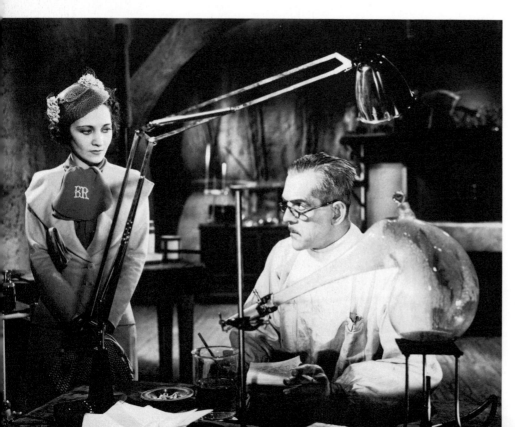

With Joan Wyndham.

Charlie Chan at the Opera

20th Century–Fox   1937.

CREDITS

Directed by H. Bruce Humberstone. *Screenplay by* W. Scott Darling *and* Charles S. Belden. *Based on the Charlie Chan stories by* Earl Derr Biggers. *Photography,* Lucien Andriot. *Editor,* Alex Troffey. Released January 8, 1937. Running time: 67 minutes.

CAST

Warner Oland, Boris Karloff, Keye Luke, Charlotte Henry, Thomas Beck, Margaret Irving, Gregory Gaye, Nedda Harrigan, Frank Conroy, Guy Usher, William Demarest, Maurice Cass and Tom McGuire.

With Charlotte Henry.

With Warner Oland.

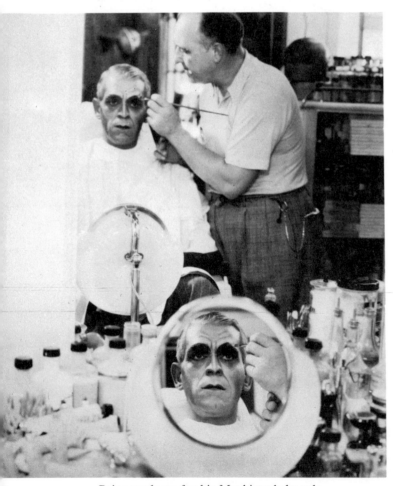

Being made up for his Mephistopheles role.

SYNOPSIS

The world had presumed the great operatic baritone, Gravelle (Boris Karloff), had died in a theatre fire. But the singer survived the holocaust and was later admitted to a mental asylum, unidentified and a victim of amnesia. One day, Gravelle is shocked by a newspaper photo of his wife, soprano Mme. Lilli Rochelle (Margaret Irving), arriving in town for a performance. He recalls she and her lover, Enrico Barelli (Gregory Gaye), plotted to murder him; they locked him in his dressing room, set fire to it, and left him for dead. Filled with revenge, he escapes.

After Mme. Rochelle learns her life is in danger, the famous Chinese detective, Charlie Chan (Warner Oland), is called into the case. Prior to the performance of *Faust,* members of the company are frightened by a strange figure lurking backstage wearing a Mephistopheles costume. During the performance, Mme. Rochelle and her lover, Barelli, are stabbed to death. Gravelle is immediately placed under suspicion for the murders. But Chan orders the opera to be played again and reveals the identity of the real killer.

REVIEWS

Scenario on the whole took plenty of cognizance of Karloff and fully warrants his presence. . . . As a cross between a madman and an amnesia victim, Karloff plays a role right down his alley. . . .

Variety

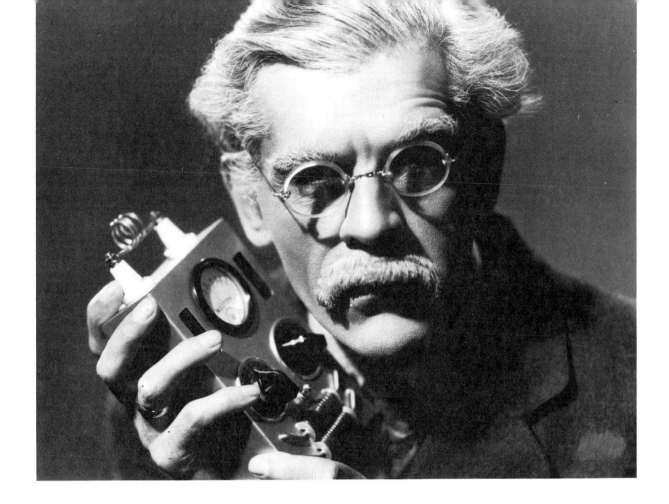

Night Key

Universal   1937.

CREDITS

Directed by Lloyd Corrigan. *Screenplay by* Tristram Tupper *and* John C. Moffit. *Photography,* George Robinson. *Editor,* Otis Garrett. *Makeup,* Jack Pierce. Released May 2, 1937. Running time: 67 minutes.

CAST

Boris Karloff, Jean Rogers, Warren Hull, Hobart Cavanaugh, Samuel Hinds, Alan Baxter, David Oliver, Edwin Maxwell, Ward Bond, Frank Reicher and Ethan Laidlaw.

SYNOPSIS

Dave Mallory (Boris Karloff) is robbed of his invention by his former partner, Ranger (Samuel Hinds), owner of a burglar alarm system company. Despite failing health, he invents a new alarm system superior to the former. Hoping to provide security for his daughter, Joan (Jean Rogers), Mallory sells it to Ranger's company on a royalty basis. But he discovers his former partner has no intention of using the new invention. Enraged, Mallory tries to force Ranger to live up to his original terms by secretly entering the stores using the system and destroying their effectiveness with his special apparatus. Realizing his business is in jeopardy, Ranger assigns his trouble-shooter, Travers (Warren Hull), to hunt down Mallory.

With Hobart Cavanaugh.

With Alan Baxter and Frank Reicher.

A gang of thieves kidnaps Mallory so they can use his invention to commit robberies. After they abduct his daughter, Mallory is forced to cooperate. Soon, the gang terrorizes the city by burglarizing every commercial establishment using Ranger's alarm system. Aided by Travers, Mallory escapes from the gang's hideout and persuades Ranger to follow his plan for capturing the criminals. After Joan is rescued and the gang rounded up by the police, Ranger promises his former partner full compensation for his invention.

REVIEW

. . . Karloff has changed. From a medieval monster he has relaxed into a soft–spoken, hazy–eyed old man who promises to become Hollywood's favorite grandpa. The change, however, has not kept him from bringing along to his new role a terrifying little gadget that shoots out Wellsian electric rays and kills off villains in a novel and exciting way.

. . . Its unfortunate that the speed of the story, one of its virtues, had to be marred by occasional time out for side romance . . .

Brooklyn Daily Eagle

With Frank Reicher, Alan Baxter, Jean Rogers, Ward Bond, Hobart Cavanaugh and Ethan Laidlaw.

126

With Ricardo Cortez, Richard Loo and Douglas Wood.

West of Shanghai

Warner Bros.   1937.

CREDITS

Directed by John Farrow. *Screenplay by* Crane Wilbur. *Based on the play by* Porter Emerson Browne. *Photography,* Lu O'Connell. *Editor,* Frank Dewar. *Makeup,* Perc Westmore. Released October 30, 1937. Running time: 65 minutes.

CAST

Boris Karloff, Beverly Roberts, Ricardo Cortez, Gordon Oliver, Sheila Bromley, Vladimir Sokoloff, Gordon Hart, Richard Loo, Douglas Wood, Chester Gan, Luke Chan, Selmer Jackson, James B. Leong, Tetsu Komai, Eddie Lee, Maurice Lui and Mia Ichioaka.

SYNOPSIS

American promoters Myron Galt (Douglas Wood) and Gordon Creed (Ricardo Cortez) arrive in a small village in the bandit–infested country of northern China. They intend to foreclose on a valuable oil concession owned by Jim Hallet (Gordon Oliver). Creed discovers his estranged wife, Jane (Beverly Roberts), a medical missionary, is in love with Hallet. But he refuses to give her a divorce. Looking for loot, an army of cutthroat bandits led by a renegade general, Wu Yen Fang (Boris Karloff), captures the town and sets up headquarters in the mission. The Americans and missionaries find themselves prisoners of the warlord and are at his mercy.

Fang remembers Hallet saved his life years ago when he was a coolie. Eager to return the favor, the warlord wipes out Hallet's debt by tearing up the foreclosure note. After discovering Creed and his companion plotting to murder Hallet, Fang shoots Creed. Government troops finally arrive and take Fang prisoner. But the warlord non-

With Beverly Roberts.

chalantly faces the firing squad knowing his friend Jim Hallet and Jane are now free to marry.

NOTES

West of Shanghai was the third filming of the Holbrook Blinn play, *The Bad Man*. In 1923, it was a silent film with Holbrook Blinn; and in the 1930 talkie version, Walter Huston repeated the role of the Mexican bandit.

Because the war in China monopolized the newspaper headlines during the '30s, Hollywood repeatedly turned to the Orient for its settings. Hoping to cash in on the present Sino–Japanese conflict, Warner Bros. transformed the Mexican locale of *The Bad Man* into the bandit country of China for *West of Shanghai*.

REVIEW

A slow–moving B . . . It has Karloff starred, but it isn't the B.K. of *Frankenstein* . . . he is burlesqued somewhat as a Chinese bandit trying to emulate the methods of American racketeers . . . his make-up being excellent, and the lightness of touch the actor is able to give the interpretation. . . . The plot is one of the absurdities almost all the way . . .

Variety

With Gordon Oliver.

128

The Invisible Menace

Warner Bros.   1938.

CREDITS

Directed by John Farrow. *Screenplay by* Crane Wilbur. *Based on the play by* Ralph Spencer Zink. *Photography,* L. William O'Connell. *Editor,* Harold McLernon. Released January 22, 1938. Running time: 56 minutes.

CAST

Boris Karloff, Marie Wilson, Eddie Craven, Eddie Acuff, Regis Toomey, Henry Kolker, Cy Kendall, Charles Trowbridge, Frank Faylen, William Haade, Harland Tucker, Phyllis Barry, John Ridgely, Jack Mower, Anderson Lawlor and John Harron.

SYNOPSIS

Following a brief leave, Pvt. Eddie Pratt (Eddie Craven) smuggles his new bride, Sally (Marie Wilson), to Powder Island Arsenal, a government reservation. Intending to hide her in an unoccupied building, they discover the mutilated body of an officer. After an investigation begins, a mysterious attempt is made on the lives of the officers in charge. Every member on the post falls under suspicion.

Realizing that their lives are in danger, the officers enlist the aid of Colonel Rogers (Cy Kendall) of the Military Intelligence. After Colonel Rogers arrives to take charge of the case, he recognizes one of the civilians, Jevries (Boris Karloff), to be an embezzler whom he arrested years before. It is also revealed that the murdered man was his enemy. As the accused man protests his innocence, the circumstantial evidence grows. But Sally accidentally stumbles upon the identity of the real murderer.

With Frank Faylen.

NOTES

Based on the 1937 Broadway play, *Without Warning,* actor Eddie Craven repeated his original stage role in *The Invisible Menace*. Warners remade the film five years later as *Murder on the Waterfront*. In this forty–nine–minute programmer, John Loder was cast in the Karloff role.

REVIEW

It's beginning to look . . . as though Boris (ex-Frankenstein) Karloff has deliberately renounced his title as the screen's Number One bogie man. Once a symbol of hair–raising jitters, he pops up . . . as the star of *The Invisible Menace*.

But a close observer . . . can see that . . . his role is a sympathetic one . . . free of sinister significance. Customers . . . expecting to be scared will find themselves feeling sorry for him.

New York Journal-American

With Cy Kendall, Regis Toomey, Henry Kolker, Eddie Craven, Marie Wilson and Charles Trowbridge.

Mr. Wong, Detective

Monogram   1938.

CREDITS

Directed by William Nigh. *Produced by* Scott R. Dunlap. *Screenplay by* Houston Branch. *Based on the stories by* Hugh Wiley. *Photography,* Harry Neumann. *Editor,* Russell Schoengarth. *Makeup,* Gordon Bau. Released October 5, 1938. Running time: 69 minutes.

CAST

Boris Karloff, Grant Withers, Maxine Jennings, Evelyn Brent, Lucien Prival, William Gould, John Hamilton, Tchin, John St. Polis, Hooper Atchley, Frank Bruno and George Lloyd.

SYNOPSIS

Dayton (John Hamilton), a chemical manufacturer, receives anonymous threats on his life after his company began manufacturing a dangerous poison gas. He visits the famous Chinese detective, James Lee Wong (Boris Karloff), who promises to help him. The following day, Dayton is slain by poison gas. Soon, two of Dayton's business partners also mysteriously die from the gas.

The mystery deepens as Wong and Capt. Street (Grant Withers) of the San Francisco police encounter a gang of international spies who desire the formula of the poison gas for a foreign government. The Chinese detective discovers the gas was ingeniously enclosed in a glass bulb which shattered from vibration. Wong eventually reveals the murderer to be the inventor of the gas who suspected that the murdered men were swindling him.

NOTES

Hoping to duplicate the success of the current Oriental detective craze (Charlie Chan, Mr. Moto) on the screen, Monogram acquired the screen rights to the Mr. Wong short stories by Hugh Wiley in *Collier's* magazine. After testing several character actors like Harold Huber, producer Dunlap approached Karloff for the Wong role. With horror films temporarily on the wane, Karloff signed for four films and hoped the success of the series might encourage producers to cast him in other straight roles.

Mr. Wong, Detective was later remade as a

Charlie Chan film, *Docks of New Orleans* (with Roland Winters in the starring role) in 1948.

REVIEW

Producers . . . intend making a sleuth out of Karloff and continuing him in a group of features concerning his Sherlockian activities. But a better job will have to be done than on this initial attempt if the series lives up to its potentialities. First picture suffers from directorial and writing troubles, plus a combination of careless acting and haphazard casting. Despite these handicaps, Karloff shows he is suited for this new type role and doesn't need a grotesque makeup to register. Regret on this initial opus that more care was not used in handling intrigue elements . . .

Karloff fights vigorously to make his character stand out, despite lagging story buildup and action . . .

"Wear," *Variety*

With Evelyn Brent, Lucien Prival and Frank Bruno.

132

With Bela Lugosi and Basil Rathbone.

Son of Frankenstein

Universal   1939.

CREDITS

Directed by Rowland V. Lee. *Produced by* Rowland V. Lee. *Screenplay by* Willis Cooper. *Photography*, George Robinson. *Editor,* Ted Kent. *Musical score,* Frank Skinner. *Makeup,* Jack Pierce. Released January 13, 1939. Running time: 94 minutes.

CAST

Basil Rathbone, Boris Karloff, Bela Lugosi, Lionel Atwill, Josephine Hutchinson, Emma Dunn, Donnie Dunagan, Edgar Norton, Perry Ivins, Lawrence Grant, Lionel Belmore, Michael Mark, Caroline Cook, Tom Ricketts, Lorimer Johnson, Gustav von Seyffertitz, Jack Harris, Betty Chay, Edward Cassidy, Ward Bond and Harry Cording.

SYNOPSIS

Twenty-five years after his father's death, Baron Wolf von Frankenstein (Basil Rathbone), his wife (Josephine Hutchinson) and young son, Peter (Donnie Dunagan), return to the family ancestral home. Believing the young scientist and his family to be in danger, Inspector Krogh (Lionel Atwill) offers his protection. Frankenstein learns that six villagers were mysteriously murdered and the slayings were never solved. While investigating his father's old laboratory, he encounters Ygor (Bela Lugosi), a crazed, deformed shepherd who survived a hanging sentence for grave-robbing. In the secret family crypt, Frankenstein learns the Monster (Boris Karloff) is still alive, but in a coma.

With Bela Lugosi.

With Basil Rathbone.

Anxious to vindicate his father's name, Frankenstein decides to revive the Monster with electrical energy. After regaining consciousness, the Monster falls under Ygor's evil influence and systematically murders the remaining jurors who sentenced the shepherd to death. Suspecting the worst, Frankenstein tries to kill the Monster, but Ygor prevents this. Later, the scientist kills the shepherd in self-defense. Grief-stricken, the Monster kidnaps Peter, intending to kill him. But Frankenstein arrives at the last moment to rescue his son and kicks the brute into the nearby boiling sulphur pit. His father's creation apparently destroyed, Frankenstein leaves the continent to begin life anew with his family.

NOTES

For Karloff's last film for Universal as the Frankenstein Monster, Willis Cooper, creator of the radio show *Lights Out,* wrote the original screenplay.

After acquiring the British-made color film,

With Basil Rathbone, Edgar Norton and Bela Lugosi.

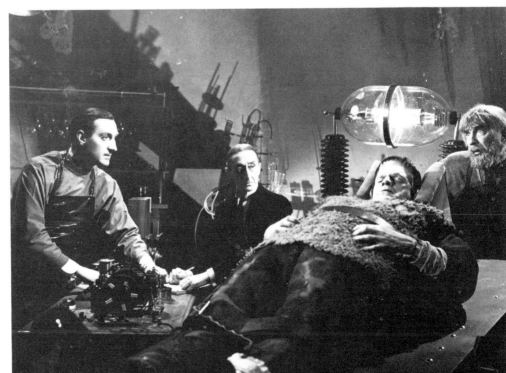

With Lionel Atwill and Donnie
Dunagan.

The Mikado, the studio decided to make *Son of Frankenstein* Universal's first feature in Technicolor. But after shooting began in October 1938, it was discovered that Karloff's makeup didn't photograph properly in color. Dwight Frye was included in abandoned color footage and the entire film was finally shot in black and white instead. *Son of Frankenstein* proved so successful, it launched the horror film cycle which lasted until the late 1940s.

REVIEWS

. . . Picture is well mounted, nicely directed, and includes cast of capable artists. Karloff has his Monster in former groove as the big and powerful brute who crushes and smashes victims . . .

Universal has given "A" production layout to the thriller in all departments. Story is slow and draggy in getting under way prior to first appearance of Karloff, but from that point on, sustains interest at high pitch.

Variety

With Bela Lugosi.

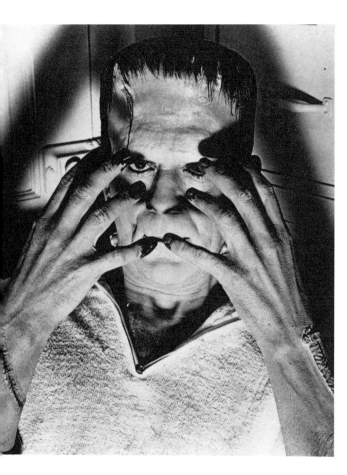

Artistically, *Son of Frankenstein* is a masterpiece in the demonstration of how production settings and effects can be made assets emphasizing literary melodrama. Histrionically, the picture is outstanding because of the manner in which Basil Rathbone, Boris Karloff, Bela Lugosi and Lionel Atwill . . . sink their teeth into their roles.

Motion Picture Herald

If Boris Karloff could scare the pants off the public when he appeared . . . as the Monster in *Frankenstein,* he'll most likely have it jumping out of its shirt with fright in the third of the . . . series . . . Rowland V. Lee has created an eerie atmosphere for the story and he has put into the working out of the plot enough horror to send the chills and shivers racing up and down the spectators' backs. For its type, the new horror film is well done.

Kate Cameron, *New York Daily News*

Celebrating his 51st birthday on the set with Basil Rathbone, Director Rowland V. Lee and Bela Lugosi.

With Joe Devlin, Jack Kennedy and Grant Withers (kneeling).

The Mystery of Mr. Wong

Monogram   1939.

CREDITS

Directed by William Nigh. *Screenplay by* W. Scott Darling. *Based on the stories by* Hugh Wiley. *Photography,* Harry Neumann. *Editor,* Russell Schoengarth. *Makeup,* Gordon Bau. Released March 8, 1939. Running time: 68 minutes.

CAST

Boris Karloff, Grant Withers, Dorothy Tree, Lotus Long, Morgan Wallace, Holmes Herbert, Craig Reynolds, Ivan Lebedeff, Hooper Atchley, Lee Tong Foo and Chester Gan.

With Morgan Wallace.

SYNOPSIS

Brandon Edwards (Morgan Wallace), gem collector, gains possession of the largest star sapphire in the world, the "Eye of the Daughter of the Moon," stolen from China. While proudly exhibiting the precious gem at a party in his home, Edwards confides in Mr. Wong (Boris Karloff) his life is in danger. During a game of charades, the host is mysteriously shot dead and the gem disappears. Unknown to the Chinese detective, the jewel is in the possession of the maid, Drina (Lotus Long), who plans to return it to its original resting place. But Drina is murdered also.

After another murder, Wong finally exposes his old friend, Professor Janney (Holmes Herbert), as the killer. After turning him over to Capt. Street (Grant Withers), he returns the "Eye of the Daughter of the Moon" to China.

REVIEW

Fairly engrossing murder mystery . . . On occasion the lack of action makes the continuity tiresome . . .

Karloff is considerably out of character but very effective as the Oriental sleuth. . . . For years he has been built up as a horror character with gymnastics and a voice to suit. Here, as Wong, Karloff is more the drawing-room type, carefully choosing his words and employing as fine diction as he has at his command . . .

"Char," *Variety*

Mr. Wong in Chinatown

Monogram   1939.

CREDITS

Directed by William Nigh. *Screenplay by* W. Scott Darling. *Based on the stories by* Hugh Wiley. *Photography,* Harry Neumann. *Editor,* Russell Schoengarth. *Makeup,* Gordon Bau. Released August 1, 1939. Running time: 70 minutes.

CAST

Boris Karloff, Grant Withers, Marjorie Reynolds, Peter George Lynn, William Royle, Huntly Gordon, James Flavin, Lotus Long, Richard Loo, Bessie Loo, Lee Tong Foo, Angelo Rosita and Guy Usher.

SYNOPSIS

Princess Lin Hwa (Lotus Long) visits Mr. Wong (Boris Karloff) in his home for help, but she is killed by a poisoned arrow. Wong, with Capt. Street (Grant Withers), seeks the murderer. They are joined by Bobby Logan (Marjorie Reynolds), reporter and Street's fiancee. Arriving at the princess's apartment to look for clues, they discover that her maid has been murdered. The only witness to the murder is a mute dwarf (Angelo Rosita) who mysteriously disappears.

Wong learns that the princess was murdered for the money she transported here to buy airplanes for her homeland. On the trail of a suspect, Wong falls into his clutches, but he is rescued by Street and Bobby. The Chinese detective discovers the murderer to be Davidson (Huntly Gordon), manager of the bank in which the royal lady's money was deposited.

REVIEW

. . . (Karloff's) treatment of the part is typed by now and he handles the characterization no differently than he did in other pictures in the series . . .

Picture lacks excitement for the most part and redeems itself only in the last half. Karloff is unduly calm and unruffled no matter what happens. His role could have stood more wallop and action . . .

Variety

With Grant Withers and Angelo
Rosita.

With William Royle, Huntly Gordon
and Peter George Lynn.

The Man
They Could Not Hang

Columbia   1939.

CREDITS

Directed by Nick Grinde. *Screenplay by* Karl
Brown. *Based on a story by* Leslie T. White *and*
George W. Sayre. *Photography,* Benjamin Kline.
Editor, William Lyon. Released August 17, 1939.
Running time: 65 minutes.

CAST

Boris Karloff, Lorna Gray, Robert Wilcox, Roger
Pryor, Don Beddoe, Ann Doran, Joseph DeStef-
ani, Charles Trowbridge, Byron Foulger, Dick
Curtis, James Craig and John Tyrrell.

SYNOPSIS

Dr. Savaard (Boris Karloff) creates a mechanical
heart designed to bring life back to the dead. In
order to test his machine, he puts a volunteer student to death. His assistant, Betty Crawford (Ann
Doran), informs the police. Refusing to believe

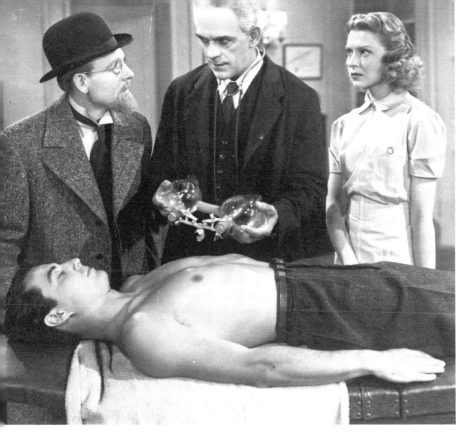

With Stanley Brown (on table), Byron Foulger and Ann Doran.

he can restore the student to life, the authorities place Savaard under arrest. The doctor is convicted of murder and sentenced to death by hanging. His faithful assistant, Lang (Byron Foulger), claims his body from prison and restores him back to life with the mechanical heart. Consumed with revenge, Savaard determines to murder everyone responsible for his conviction at the trial. He methodically murders six jurors under conditions resembling suicide.

The remainder of the trial forces are duped into entering Savaard's home, which is rigged with lethal booby traps. After several die by electricity and poison, Savaard's daughter, Janet (Lorna Gray), arrives and attempts to free his prisoners, but she is electrocuted. While Savaard attempts to restore her back to life, the police burst in, mortally wounding him. After her life is restored, Savaard destroys his invention and dies.

The execution scene.

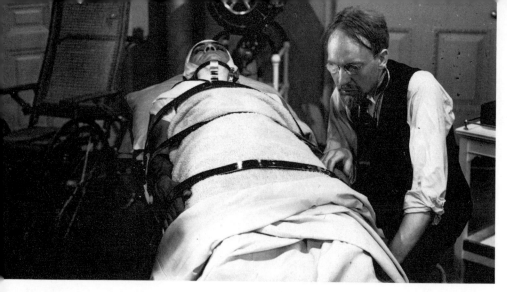

With Byron Foulger

NOTES

The storyline of *The Man They Could Not Hang* was inspired by actual experiments conducted by Dr. Robert Cornish. The biochemist attracted publicity during the thirties by restoring dead dogs back to life after gassing them with nitrogen gas. Cornish also tried to obtain permission to restore life to executed convicts in order to further test his theories. But he did not obtain the opportunity to do so.

The film's success encouraged Columbia to sign Karloff for several more films in the same theme, launching the actor onto his second "crazed scientist" cycle which lasted until Karloff returned to the stage in early 1941.

Ironically, Karloff's experiments in restoring life to the dead with a mechanical heart antici- pated similar medical advances in real life. More than twenty-five years later, human lives were successfully prolonged by surgical heart trans- plants.

REVIEW

Boris Karloff looks less menacing than he has been in the past, but while he is a complacent, kindly type of character part of the way . . . he ends up on a rather sinister note . . .

Plot is inconsistent with the deep interest of Karloff in promoting life by his discovery to delib- erately turn murderer in the end. The unexpected and implausible revenge doesn't jell, but Karloff turns in his usual good performance . . .

"Char," *Variety*

With Dick Curtis, John Tyrrell, Robert Wilcox, Don Beddoe, Ann Doran, Charles Trowbridge, Roger Pryor, Joseph DeStefani and James Craig.

Tower of London

Universal   1939.

CREDITS

Directed by Rowland V. Lee. *Screenplay by* Robert N. Lee. *Photography,* George Robinson. *Editor,* Ed Curtiss. *Musical score,* Frank Skinner. *Makeup,* Jack Pierce. Released November 17, 1939. Running time: 92 minutes.

CAST

Basil Rathbone, Boris Karloff, Barbara O'Neil, Ian Hunter, Vincent Price, Nan Grey, John Sutton, Leo G. Carroll, Miles Mander, Lionel Belmore, Rose Hobart, Ralph Forbes, Frances Robinson, Ernest Cossart, G. P. Huntley, John Rodion, Ronald Sinclair, John Herbert Bond, Donnie Dunagan, Ernie Adams, Harry Cording, C. Montague Shaw, Ivan Simpson and Nigel de Brulier.

As Mord in the torture chamber sequence.

SYNOPSIS

In fifteenth–century England, Lord DeVere (John Rodion) is executed for treason by King Edward IV (Ian Hunter). John Wyatt's (John Sutton) loyalty to his cousin and refusal to enter a planned marriage to strengthen the royal ties arouses the displeasure of Edward and his younger brother Richard, Duke of Gloucester (Basil Rathbone). He is imprisoned in the Tower. Hoping the aging Henry VI (Miles Mander) will be slain, Edward and Richard bring the imbecilic King with them to meet the Prince of Wales in the Battle of Tewkesbury. But Henry survives and is murdered by Mord (Boris Karloff), executioner and Richard's ally. After killing Wales in battle, Richard covets Anne Neville (Rose Hobart), the slain

man's wife. But Clarence (Vincent Price), brother of Edward and Richard, tries to prevent this and arranges to have Anne hidden away. Mord's spies locate her and she is tricked into marrying Richard. Soon, Richard drowns Clarence in a huge wine barrel.

After King Edward dies, his eldest son, Prince Edward (Ronald Sinclair), is crowned king. Under Richard's orders, Mord murders the boy king and his brother in the Tower. Now King of England, Richard tries to prevent the stolen royal treasure from reaching Tudor in France. But Wyatt transports the treasure to the exiled King. With a new army, Tudor returns to England and meets Richard and Mord at the Battle of Bos-

With Basil Rathbone and Vincent Price.

With Basil Rathbone.

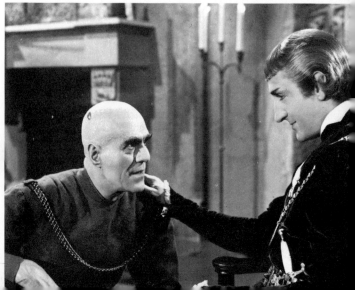

With John Herbert–Bond and
Ronald Sinclair.

worth. King Richard and Mord are slain and Tudor is then proclaimed King.

NOTES

Rowland V. Lee hoped to repeat the success of his *Son of Frankenstein* earlier that year, by re-uniting Karloff and Rathbone in the lively fifteenth–century melodrama, *Tower of London.* In spite of its factual pretensions, Lee deliberately simplified historical incidents and carried off each gruesome beheading, drowning, stabbing, etc. in the manner of a Karloff–Lugosi vehicle. To this Grand Guignol bloodbath, he also reused the musical score from *Son of Frankenstein,* repeating the Monster theme for Karloff.

In spite of its impressive–looking production qualities, Lee shrewdly concealed its actual low–budget economy: During the location shooting of its battle scenes at Tarzana in California, the cardboard helmets and armor worn by the extras became hopelessly soggy after the rain machines were turned on. Inevitably, the scenes had to be reshot. Some of the standing sets in *Tower of London* turned up later in the serial *Flash Gordon Conquers the Universe* and in *Horror Island.*

Coincidentally, one of the actors in *Tower of London* repeated Rathbone's role over two decades later. In 1962, Vincent Price played Richard III in the United Artists production of the same name. Basil Rathbone's son, who had a brief fling in films, appeared in the 1939 version under the name of John Rodion.

Clowning on the set with John
Rodion and Basil Rathbone.

147

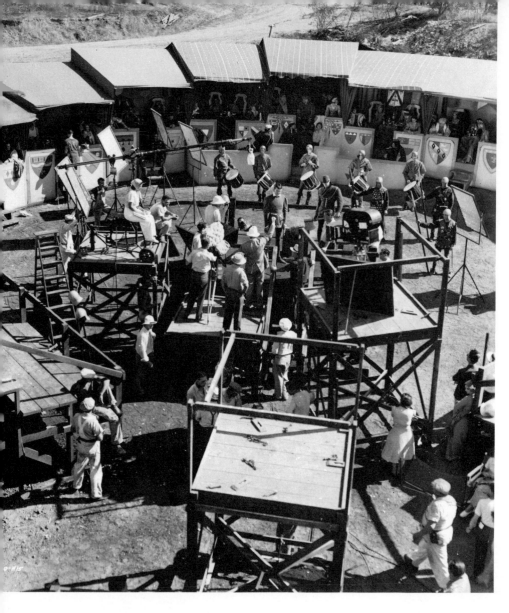

Director Rowland V. Lee (arm up-raised) prepares to shoot a scene with the cast.

REVIEWS

... As a horror picture, it's one of the most broadly etched, but still so strong it may provide disturbing nightmares as aftermath ...

Rathbone provides a most vivid portrayal ... Karloff is familiar ... Rowland Lee has directed deftly, neatly mixing his dramatic ingredients for suspenseful values.

Variety

... Director Rowland Lee and his Scripter–Brother Robert N. Lee claim they boned through 350 volumes of British history ... this period thriller is less authentic than its elaborately spooky reproductions of London's Tower. But the battles of Tewkesbury and Bosworth ... set a new high

for realistic racket that should deafen the most demanding.

Best shot: Richard and Mord drowning the Duke of Clarence, Richard's brother, in a vast butt of malmsey ... with beautifully bubbling sound effects.

Time

Tower of London is as sinister as Basil Rathbone, Boris Karloff and the rest of Universal's horror department can make it ...

Although the picture is not without its weaknesses, lack of thrills is not one of them. Neither is the casting ... Rathbone and Karloff ... are savage enough to please the most bloodthirsty ...

Dorothy Masters, New York *Daily News*

With Tristram Coffin, Lita Cheveret and Grant Withers.

The Fatal Hour

Monogram   1940.

CREDITS

Directed by William Nigh. *Screenplay by* W. Scott Darling. *Based on the stories by* Hugh Wiley. *Photography,* Harry Neumann. *Editor,* Russell Schoengarth. *Makeup,* Gordon Bau. Released January 15, 1940. Running time: 68 minutes.

CAST

Boris Karloff, Grant Withers, Marjorie Reynolds, Charles Trowbridge, John Hamilton, Craig Reynolds, Jack Kennedy, Lita Cheveret, Frank Puglia, Stanford Jolley, Jason Robards Sr. and Pauline Drake.

SYNOPSIS

Unable to track down the murderer of his best friend, Detective Dan O'Grady, Capt. Street (Grant Withers), asks Mr. Wong (Boris Karloff) to assist him on the case. The slain detective had been trying to solve a smuggling case. As the Chinese detective tracks down various suspects including a jewelry store operator and a nightclub owner, three more murders occur. With the aid of reporter Bobby Logan (Marjorie Reynolds), Wong and Capt. Street apprehend the murderer, Forbes (Charles Trowbridge), at the last moment.

REVIEW

A routine murder mystery, none too well produced, which has as its principal saving grace the suave Boris Karloff . . . as a master detective. Basically an ordinary story, its failure to impress is largely due to the elemental plot and the inconsistencies which figure . . .

"Char," *Variety*

With Richard Loo.

149

British Intelligence

Warner Bros. 1940.

CREDITS

Directed by Terry Morse. *Screenplay by* Lee Katz. *Based on the play by* Anthony Paul Kelly. *Photography,* Sid Hickox. *Editor,* Thomas Pratt. *Makeup,* Perc Westmore. Released January 29, 1940. Running time: 62 minutes.

CAST

Boris Karloff, Margaret Lindsay, Maris Wrixon, Bruce Lester, Leonard Mudie, Holmes Herbert, Winifred Harris, Lester Matthews, John Graham Spacy, Austin Fairman, Clarence Derwent, Louise Brien, Frederick Vogeding, Carlos de Valdez, Frederick Giermann, Willy Kaufman and Frank Mayo.

SYNOPSIS

During World War I, Helene von Lorbeer (Margaret Lindsay), a nurse in a French hospital, as-

With Margaret Lindsay.

sumes the role of a German spy and is instructed to go to England. There, she must obtain important information concerning a secret British offensive. Through the efforts of an Englishman in the pay of the Germans, Helene is accepted as a guest in the household of Arthur Bennett (Holmes Herbert), an important British war official. She learns Valdar (Boris Karloff), the butler, is a German spy also and that she will be receiving instructions from him. Helene tries to learn the identity of Schiller, the mastermind of the German spy system, but Valdar prevents this.

Suspecting she is a British agent, Valdar lures her to the basement of the house, intending to kill her. But she convinces him otherwise and discovers he is the spy chieftain, Schiller. Learning of an important cabinet meeting to take place in the house, Schiller plans to destroy every member with a time bomb. But his scheme is foiled and the master spy is shot down while escaping the British authorities.

NOTES

Anthony Paul Kelly's play, *Three Faces East,* was filmed twice before under this same title. In 1926, the first filming featured Clive Brook and Jetta Goudal; in the 1930 remake, the cast starred Eric von Stroheim and Constance Bennett. In this third version, Karloff recreated Stroheim's spy role.

REVIEW

Boris Karloff, sans grotesque makeup, and Margaret Lindsay help vastly in making this remake of *Three Faces East* exciting. . . . The 1940 version should generate nice box office because of Karloff and the current European war.

Karloff makes a juicy morsel of the German spy role, depending almost entirely on his acting ability to impress. He has a supposed bayonet wound on his face, walks with a limp and is the picture's menace because of his sheer trouping.

"Wear," *Variety*

151

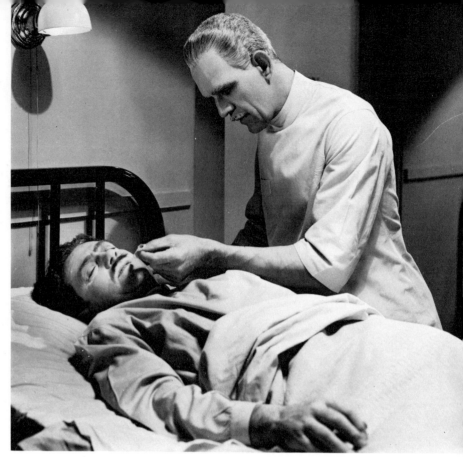

With Stanley Ridges.

Black Friday

Universal   1940.

CREDITS

Directed by Arthur Lubin. *Screenplay by* Curt Siodmak *and* Eric Taylor. *Photography,* Elwood Bredell. *Editor,* Phillip Cahn. *Musical score,* Hans J. Salter. Released April 12, 1940. Running time: 70 minutes.

CAST

Boris Karloff, Bela Lugosi, Stanley Ridges, Ann Nagel, Anne Gwynne, Virginia Brissac, Edmund MacDonald, Paul Fix, Murray Alper, Ray Bailey, Jack Mulhall, Joe King and John Kelly.

SYNOPSIS

During a street battle between gangsters, George Kingsley (Stanley Ridges), a college professor, is injured. He and a notorious gangster, Red Cannon, are rushed to a hospital. Hoping to save his friend Kingsley, Dr. Sovac (Boris Karloff) transplants part of Cannon's brain to Kingsley's. The operation is a success; Kingsley lives, but Cannon dies. Hoping to learn the whereabouts of the $500,000 loot Cannon secreted from his rival, Marnay (Bela Lugosi), Sovac persuades the recuperating Kingsley to accompany him to New York. After Sovac hypnotizes him, Kingsley is transformed into Red Cannon and goes on a killing spree, killing Marnay's men. He also visits Sunny Rogers (Ann Nagel), Cannon's girlfriend, and frightens her with knowledge of secrets she shared alone with Cannon.

While Cannon retrieves his hidden loot, Mar-

With Stanley Ridges.

nay attempts to steal it and split it with Sunny, but they fail. Cannon strangles the double-crossing Sunny and cold-bloodedly suffocates Marnay to death. After the gangster changes back to Kingsley, Sovac returns home with the loot. But Kingsley suddenly reverts to Cannon again. Believing Sovac's daughter to have stolen his loot, Cannon attempts to murder her. Horrified, Sovac is forced to kill him. Before going to the electric chair, Sovac gives his diary to a reporter, believing he made a contribution to science.

NOTES

Lugosi was originally cast in the Kingsley/Can-

With Stanley Ridges.

non role. But Director Lubin scrapped his already shot footage and replaced him with actor Stanley Ridges instead. Lugosi was then given the only other role of any consequence available: Marnay.

Fully aware that this would eliminate any scenes between Karloff and Lugosi entirely, Producer Burt Kelly attempted to add a bizarre note to Lugosi's lesser role; Universal's publicity department announced that realism would be injected into Lugosi's death scene. The actor submitted himself to the powers of a professional hypnotist, Manly P. Hall, on the set in the presence of the crew and newspapermen. But in spite of this publicity gimmick and Universal's playing it up as another Karloff–Lugosi film, the vehicle turned out to be in reality a Karloff–Ridges film (with Ridges dramatically walking off with the whole film).

Curt Siodmak's script *Black Friday* coincidentally, bore more than a passing resemblance to his story *Donovan's Brain* which was later

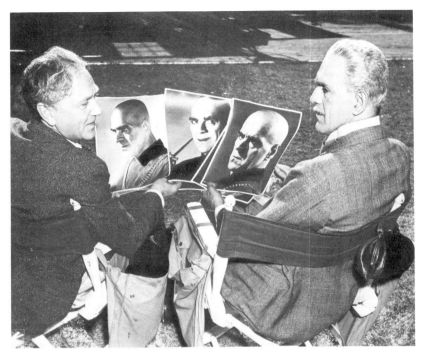

With Stanley Ridges on the set.

filmed twice. Though *Black Friday* wasn't the last of the Karloff–Lugosi vehicles, it was their last together for Universal.

REVIEW

. . . Despite its incredulity, contains sufficient chiller content to amply satisfy addicts of this type of entertainment.

. . . Screenplay, in straining to achieve surprise shocks for audience attention, lacks smoothness in its setup.

Karloff plays the scientist straight, but gains little audience sympathy with his mercenary attitude combined with his drive for a new scientific discovery . . .

Variety

With Bela Lugosi and chorines on the nightclub set.

155

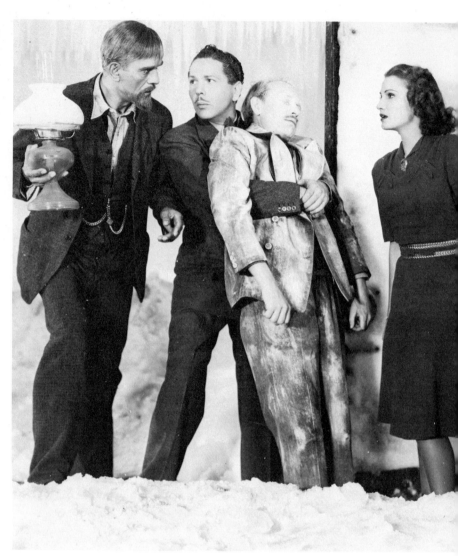

With Roger Pryor, Byron Foulger and Jo Ann Sayers.

The Man with Nine Lives

Columbia   1940.

CREDITS

Directed by Nick Grinde. *Screenplay by* Karl Brown. *Based on a story by* Harold Shumate. *Photography,* Benjamin Kline. *Editor,* Al Clark. Released April 18, 1940. Running time: 73 minutes.

CAST

Boris Karloff, Roger Pryor, Jo Ann Sayers, Stanley Brown, John Dilson, Hal Taliaferro, Byron Foulger, Charles Trowbridge and Ernie Adams.

SYNOPSIS

Believing he can cure cancer by freezing, Dr. Kravaal (Boris Karloff) places his dying patient in an underground ice chamber carved out from a surrounding glacier. The patient's nephew, Bob Adams (Stanley Brown), and local officials visit Kravaal's laboratory, believing his patient to be a victim of foul play. Realizing his patient will die if he is arrested, Kravaal tries to frighten his captors away with a powerful drug. In the confusion, the drug renders Kravaal and the rest unconscious.

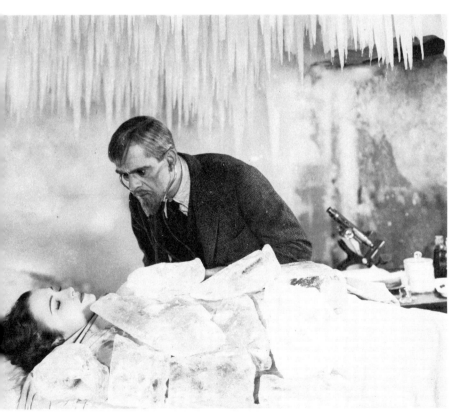

With Jo Ann Sayers.

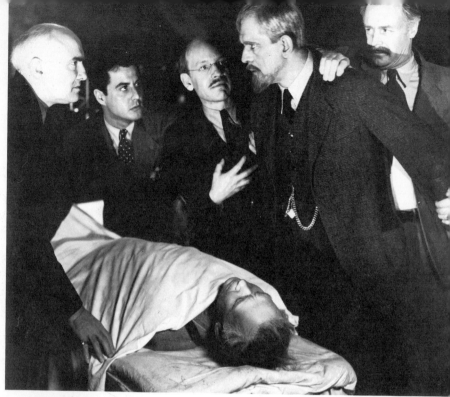

With John Dilson, Stanley Brown, Byron Foulger and Hal Taliaferro.

Ten years after the mysterious disappearance of Dr. Kravaal, Dr. Tim Mason (Roger Pryor) and his assistant, Judith Blair (Jo Ann Sayers), arrive in the small Canadian village, seeking records of the doctor's experiments. They discover the ice chamber containing the frozen bodies of Dr. Kravaal and the others. After they are revived from their long sleep, Kravaal realizes the drug is the solution to the cancer cure. But Bob Adams, in sheer frustration, destroys the formula. With Mason's assistance, Kravaal makes the rest his prisoners and uses them as his guinea pigs until he obtains the complete formula. After they die from his experiments, the crazed doctor attempts to experiment on Miss Blair. But a search party reaches the ice chamber in time. Kravaal is shot, but dies knowing Mason will use his research findings for the good of mankind.

REVIEW

...*The Man with Nine Lives* is not as horrendous as some have been, but it is unusual and interesting to a certain degree.

...Karloff's makeup isn't frightening, but his acting is like a snake charming a bird.

Wanda Hale, New York *Daily News*

With Director Nick Grinde on the set.

158

Devil's Island

Warner Bros.   1940.

CREDITS

Directed by William Clemens. *Screenplay by* Kenneth Gamet *and* Don Ryan. *Based on a story by* Anthony Coldewey *and* Raymond L. Schrock. *Photography,* George Barnes. *Editor,* Frank Magee. Released July 1940. Running time: 62 minutes.

CAST

Boris Karloff, Nedda Harrigan, James Stephenson, Adia Kuznetzoff, Rolla Gourvitch, Will Stanton, Edward Keane, Robert Warwick, Pedro de Cordoba, Tom Wilson, John Harmon, Richard Bond, Earl Gunn, George Lloyd and Stuart Holmes.

SYNOPSIS

After treating a wounded political revolutionary, Dr. Gaudet (Boris Karloff), a respected brain surgeon, is unjustly sentenced to ten years' imprisonment on Devil's Island. After his arrival on the notorious penal colony, Gaudet arouses the

With Dick Rich.

With Earl Dwire (Right).

displeasure of the unsympathetic commandant, Col. Lucien (James Stephenson). Angered by inhuman conditions, Gaudet leads an unsuccessful revolt. As punishment, the commandant sentences the doctor and his captured comrades to death. After the commandant's daughter receives a head injury in a runaway accident, the commandant's wife (Nedda Harrigan) forces her husband to ask Gaudet to save their daughter's life. Accepting the commandant's promise that they will not be executed, the doctor agrees to operate. But the commandant breaks his word in spite of the operation's success.

Angered by her husband's decision, Madame Lucien arranges for Gaudet and the others to escape, but they are recaptured. Sentenced to death, Gaudet is rescued through the efforts of Madame Lucien, who convinces the governor to stop the execution. Col. Lucien is also arrested on charges of corruption. As Gaudet is freed, a new regime promises reforms on the island.

NOTES

Devil's Island had been in the planning stage since 1937 after the French government proclaimed it was going to stop using the island as a penal colony. Originally titled *Song of Hell,* Producer Bryan Foy (who later made *Blackwell's Island* which was a study of corruption uncovered at

With James Stephenson and Nedda Harrigan.

Welfare Island) had slated George Raft for the starring role. Later, Karloff was given the lead role instead after the studio decided to shelve its plans to star him in *Witches' Sabbath* because of declining public interest in horror films.

However, France decided not to eliminate the notorious colony and attacked the film as anti–French at the preview in January 1939. They immediately banned all future Warner Bros. films. The studio did not want any repetition of losses from upcoming films like *Zola* which France boycotted two years earlier, and hurriedly withdrew all prints from circulation, reshooting many scenes. After one more abortive release and more cuts, Warner Bros. officially released it over a year later. But by this time, France was too busy with World War II to object.

REVIEWS

. . . Intrinsically it is just another meller of the dreadful isle down in the Caribbean.

The story . . . is of the most obvious character and in some respects overdrawn . . . Boris Karloff plays the lead convincingly, making himself as pathetic a character as possible . . .

"Char," *Variety*

It is being touted as an "uncensored" version. But there is nothing in it that could startle a well–protected child of seven or give pause even to a censor . . .

. . . This picture sort of reminds you of a secondhand Dreyfus Case with the politics out and only the suffering left. It's not quite enough.

New York Post

161

Doomed to Die

Monogram   1940.

CREDITS

Directed by William Nigh. *Screenplay by* Ralph G. Bettinson *and* Michael Jacoby. *Based on the stories by* Hugh Wiley. *Photography,* Harry Neumann. *Editor,* Robert Golden. *Makeup,* Gordon Bau. Released August 12, 1940. Running time: 68 minutes.

CAST

Boris Karloff, Grant Withers, Marjorie Reynolds,

With Grant Withers and Guy Usher.

Melvin Lang, Guy Usher, Catherine Craig, William Sterling, Henry Brandon and Wilbur Mack.

SYNOPSIS

Shipping magnate Cyrus Wentworth (Melvin Lang) is mysteriously murdered after one of his ships containing over a million dollars in bonds is sunk. Because young Dick Fleming (William Sterling), son of the magnate's rival, was the last person to see him alive, Capt. Street (Grant Withers) arrests him for murder. Believing Dick Fleming to be innocent, reporter Bobby Logan (Marjorie Reynolds) persuades Mr. Wong (Boris Karloff) to help clear him of the charges.

Wong meets an assortment of suspects including a supposedly drowned Chinese passenger who attempted to avert a tong war, a blackmailing general manager and a dismissed chauffeur. Following an attempt on the elder Fleming's life, Wong finally reveals the true murderer to Capt. Street.

REVIEW

The routine plot unfolds in so obvious a manner that one loses interest in the outcome. The production values are on the same level as they were in the other pictures in the . . . series, and the performances are on a par with the material. Most of the comedy is provoked by the bickering between a detective and a young girl who tries to outwit him . . .

Harrison's Reports

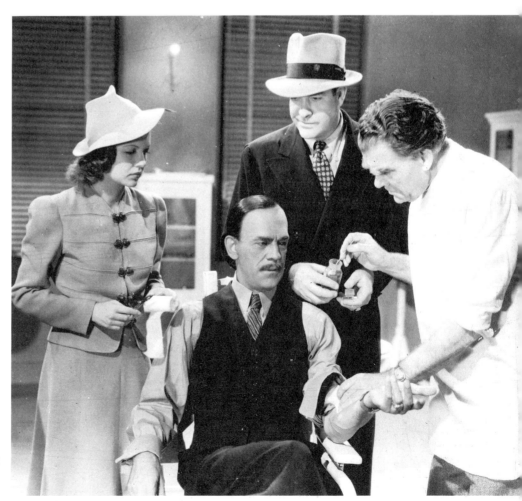

With Marjorie Reynolds, Grant Withers and Gibson Gowland.

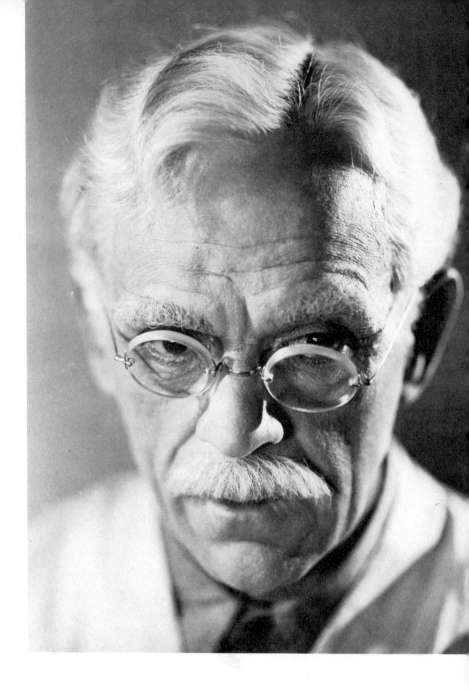

Before I Hang

Columbia   1940.

CREDITS

Directed by Nick Grinde. *Screenplay by* Robert D. Andrews. *Based on a story by* Karl Brown *and* Robert D. Andrews. *Photography,* Benjamin Kline. *Editor,* Charles Nelson. Released September 17, 1940. Running time: 63 minutes.

CAST

Boris Karloff, Evelyn Keyes, Bruce Bennett, Edward Van Sloan, Ben Taggart, Pedro de Cordoba, Wright Kramer, Bertram Marburgh, Don Beddoe, Robert Fiske, Kenneth MacDonald and Frank Richards.

With Edward Van Sloan.

With Frank Richards.

SYNOPSIS

Dr. John Garth (Boris Karloff) searches for a serum to combat old age. Unable to cure his patient suffering from the infirmities of advanced age, the doctor commits a "mercy killing." Sentenced to death by hanging, Garth is permitted to continue his experiments in prison until his execution. To insure the success of his new serum, Garth uses the blood of a condemned murderer. The serum works; after injecting himself with it, the aging doctor is transformed into a younger man. After his sentence has been changed to life imprisonment, Garth suddenly strangles the prison doctor (Edward Van Sloan). But the prison officials believe the murder was committed by another convict.

Garth is given a pardon and returns to civilian practice. Failing to persuade his aging friends to use his serum, Garth is driven to kill again. Realizing that the blood of the murderer has contaminated his mind and soul, Garth voluntarily returns to prison.

REVIEW

No matter how well Boris Karloff starts out he ends up bad . . .

The picture is fanciful pseudo-science which builds to an exciting murder orgy. Poor Boris. Once a movie murderer, always a movie murderer.

New York Post

With Wright Kramer, Pedro de Cordoba and Bertram Marburgh.

166

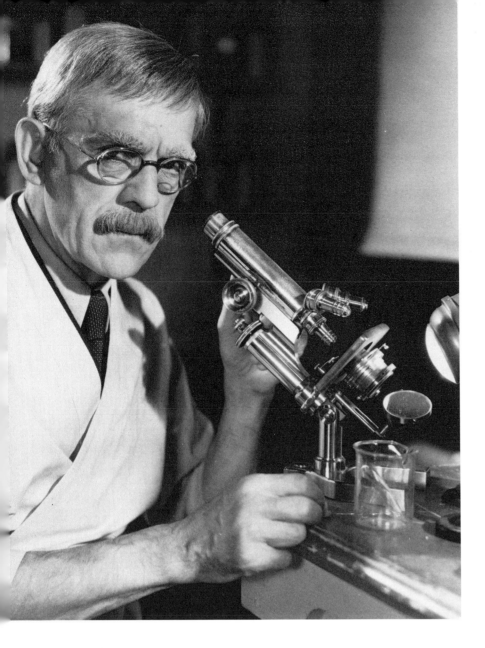

The Ape

Monogram   1940.

CREDITS

Directed by William Nigh. *Screenplay by* Curt Siodmak *and* Richard Carroll. *Based on the play by* Adam Shirk. *Photography,* Harry Neumann. *Editor,* Russell Schoengarth. *Makeup,* Gordon Bau. Released September 30, 1940. Running time: 61 minutes.

CAST

Boris Karloff, Maris Wrixon, Gertrude Hoffman, Henry Hall, Gene O'Donnell, Jack Kennedy, Jessie Arnold, I. Stanford Jolley, Selmer Jackson, Philo McCullough, Dorothy Vaughan and George Cleveland.

SYNOPSIS

After polio claims the lives of his wife and child, Dr. Adrian (Boris Karloff) dedicates his life to finding a cure for the dread disease. The only

With Gertrude Hoffman.

person in town who has faith in the doctor is Frances (Maris Wrixon), a young paralyzed woman. While trying to help her, Dr. Adrian discovers his serum will work if it contains spinal fluid from a human being. A huge ape escapes from a circus after mauling its trainer (I. Stanford Jolley). Adrian removes the spinal fluid from the mangled man. Frances' condition improves, but more fluid is needed for a complete cure. After killing the escaped ape, Adrian disguises himself in the animal's hide and sets out for more liquid for his serum.

Discovering she is still unable to walk, Adrian again sets out at night for another victim. Hunting for the escaped animal, a sheriff's posse mistakes him for the ape and mortally wounds him. Seeing this from her window, Frances rises from her wheelchair and runs to the dead doctor. His serum is a success, but the formula dies with him.

With Gene O'Donnell, Maris Wrixon and Jessie Arnold.

168

NOTES

With the advent of the horror–film cycle again, Monogram took Karloff off the Wong series and cast him in *The Ape* instead. The studio made one more Wong film (*Phantom of Chinatown*) that same year, with Keye Luke in the title role. But without Karloff in the starring role, the public lost interest in the series and it was terminated.

The Ape finished Karloff's contract with Monogram and the actor did not return to that studio until eighteen years later (Monogram became Allied Artists in 1953) to make *Frankenstein 1970*.

REVIEW

Boris Karloff is having a monster holiday....The story doesn't bear scrutiny at close range, but it does get over some good horror effects.

Kate Cameron, New York *Daily News*

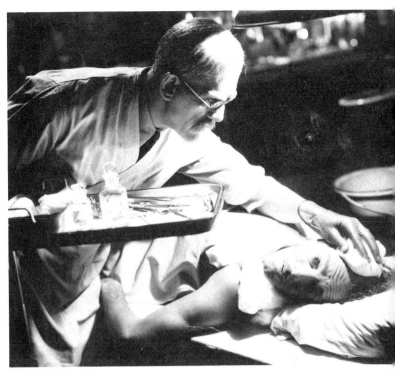

With I. Stanford Jolley.

With the escaped ape.

With Kay Kyser, Peter Lorre and Bela Lugosi.

You'll Find Out

RKO Radio   1940.

CREDITS

Directed by David Butler. *Screenplay by* James V. Kern. *Based on a story by* David Butler *and* James V. Kern. *Photography,* Frank Redman. *Editor,* Irene Morra. *Music and lyrics,* James McHugh *and* John Mercer. Released November 22, 1940. Running time: 97 minutes.

CAST

Kay Kyser, Peter Lorre, Boris Karloff, Dennis O'Keefe, Bela Lugosi, Helen Parrish, Alma Kruger, Joseph Eggenton, Ginny Simms, Harry Babbitt, Ish Kabibble and Sully Mason.

SYNOPSIS

Kay Kyser and his band are hired to provide music at the twenty–first birthday party of debutante Janis Bellacrest (Helen Parrish). Among the strange collection of guests at the gloomy Bellacrest mansion are Judge Mainwaring (Boris Karloff), Prince Saliano (Bela Lugosi) a suspicious medium, and a psychologist, Professor Fenninger (Peter Lorre). During a weird seance conducted by Saliano, Janis narrowly escapes death by a falling chandelier. After Kay and the boys do some sleuthing on their own, they discover that Saliano, Fenninger and Mainwaring

With Bela Lugosi and Peter Lorre.

are secretly working together to murder Janis to claim her inheritance.

During the next seance, Kay publicly exposes them. Attempting to escape, the trio are blown to bits in an explosion they originally planned for the guests.

REVIEWS

... Solid comedy entertainment, with musical interludes ... it generates a fast pace that carries proceedings along in zestful tempo through a maze of humorous and chiller complications.

... Boris Karloff, Bela Lugosi and Peter Lorre form a strong setup of sinister villainy ...

"Walt," *Variety*

... the script contains all the standard mystery–film props—sliding panels, secret passageways, thunder and lightning and poisoned blow–darts.

... The Messrs. Karloff, Lugosi and Lorre go in for heavy leers and obvious melodramatics of the gaslit era ...

New York Journal-American

With Ginny Simms, Helen Parrish, Peter Lorre, Bela Lugosi and Kay Kyser.

The Devil Commands

Columbia   1941.

CREDITS

Directed by Edward Dmytryk. *Screenplay by* Robert D. Andrews *and* Milton Gunzberg. *Based on the story* The Edge of Running Water *by* William Sloane. *Photography,* Allen G. Siegler. *Editor,* Al Clark. Released February 3, 1941. Running time: 65 minutes.

CAST

Boris Karloff, Richard Fiske, Amanda Duff, Anne Revere, Ralph Penney, Dorothy Adams, Walter Baldwin, Kenneth MacDonald and Shirley Warde.

SYNOPSIS

Dr. Julian Blair (Boris Karloff) fails to convince his fellow scientists that brainwaves, despite death, still live and can be electrically recorded on his machine. After his wife (Shirley Warde) dies in an automobile accident, Blair discovers she has

With Wheaton Chambers, Richard Fiske and Erwin Kalser.

been trying to send electrical impulses to him from the grave. Hoping to communicate with her, he is aided by a medium, Mrs. Walters (Anne Revere), whose body can withstand a large amount of voltage without harmful effects. During an experiment, his servant, Karl (Ralph Penney), is injured and becomes a deaf–mute. To continue his work in secrecy, they move to an old house in a remote section of New England. Nearing his goal, Blair uses bodies stolen from local grave-

yards in his experiments. One night, his maid accidentally locks herself in his laboratory and dies of fright.

Blair's daughter (Amanda Duff) arrives to persuade her father to abandon his experiments, but he forces her to carry on in the place of Mrs. Walters who was killed during a previous experiment. As her fiancee (Richard Fiske) rescues her in the nick of time, the townspeople burst into the house, bent on destruction. The laboratory appa-

With Ralph Penney and Anne Revere.

With Anne Revere.

ratus explodes, killing Dr. Blair and forever ending his dreams of communicating with the dead.

REVIEW

Concurrent with his starring Broadway stage appearance . . . in *Arsenic and Old Lace,* a murder comedy which Warners purchased last month for motion picture production . . . Karloff is seen also in a similar role in *The Devil Commands.* Produced by Columbia under the directorial guidance of Edward Dmytryk the picture, if somewhat slow, contains the necessary continuity to make it an interesting melodrama of horror and suspense.

Motion Picture Herald

With Amanda Duff.

Information Please

RKO–Pathé   1941.

Karloff appeared as guest expert in a series of ten–minute shorts based on the popular radio program. The films also contained the program's host (Clifton Fadiman), the same panelists (John Kieran, Franklin P. Adams and Oscar Levant), and used the identical format from the radio program.

With John Kieran, Franklin P. Adams and Oscar Levant.

With Maxie Rosenbloom, Peter Lorre and Frank Puglia.

The Boogie Man Will Get You

Columbia   1942.

CREDITS

Directed by Lew Landers (Louis Friedlander). *Screenplay by* Edwin Blum. *Based on a story by* Hal Fimberg *and* Robert B. Hunt. *Photography,* Henry Freulich. *Editor,* Richard Fantl. Released October 22, 1942. Running time: 66 minutes.

CAST

Boris Karloff, Peter Lorre, Maxie Rosenbloom, Jeff Donnell, Larry Parks, Maude Eburne, Don Beddoe, George McKay, Frank Puglia, Eddie Laughton, Frank Sully and James Morton.

SYNOPSIS

Prof. Nathaniel Billings (Boris Karloff) sells his old Colonial Inn to young Winnie Layden (Jeff Donnell) in return for permission to continue his experiments in the basement. Hoping to stop his ex–wife from making a bad investment, Bill Layden (Larry Parks) arrives, but it is too late. In the basement, the local sheriff and medico, Dr. Lorentz (Peter Lorre), discovers five bodies used as guinea pigs by Prof. Billings. He learns Billings is perfecting an invention which will transform ordinary men into supermen, making a vital contribution to the war effort. After Billings agrees to include Lorentz as a partner, the pair persuade a gullible salesman (Maxie Rosenbloom) to be their next guinea pig.

After Bill and Winnie discover the bodies, they call the police. Investigating the basement, they find Lorentz and Billings terrorized by an escaped Fascist (Frank Puglia), trying to pry the "superman" secret out of them. After it is revealed that the bodies are not dead, merely in a state of suspended animation, all of the occupants are rounded up and sent to the insane asylum.

NOTES

The Boogie Man Will Get You was the last film commitment Karloff owed Columbia. After a

176

With Peter Lorre.

great deal of postponement on the part of the Broadway producers of *Arsenic and Old Lace,* Karloff was permitted to leave the cast in order to join his co-star Peter Lorre in Hollywood. The film was shot in the late summer of 1942 and was deliberately fashioned to capitalize on the success of Karloff's current Broadway play.

REVIEW

The studio took Boris Karloff out of the stage cast of *Arsenic and Old Lace* to play the role of the scientific investigator.... But frightening people in theatres takes more ingenuity and adroitness than the authors of this screenplay put into it.

Kate Cameron, New York *Daily News*

With Peter Lorre, Jeff Donnell and Larry Parks.

With June Vincent.

The Climax

Universal   1944.

CREDITS

Directed by George Waggner. *Produced by* George Waggner. *Screenplay by* Curt Siodmak *and* Lynn Starling. *Based on the play by* Edward J. Locke. *Photography,* Hal Mohr *and* W. Howard Greene. *Editor,* Russell Schoengarth. *Musical score,* Edward Ward. *Color by* Technicolor. Released October 20, 1944. Running time: 86 minutes.

CAST

Boris Karloff, Susanna Foster, Turhan Bey, Gale Sondergaard, Thomas Gomez, June Vincent, George Dolenz, Ludwig Stossel, Jane Farrar, Erno Verebes, Lotte Stein, Scotty Beckett, William Edmunds, Grace Cunard, Maurice Costello, William Desmond, Stuart Holmes, Eddie Polo and Jack Richardson.

SYNOPSIS

Years ago, Dr. Hohner (Boris Karloff) ruthlessly murdered Marcellina (June Vincent), the great opera star, because her career came between them. On the tenth anniversary of her mysterious disappearance, the opera house physician learns that Angela (Susanna Foster), a young singer, has been chosen to sing *The Magic Voice*. Believing Angela's voice is a reincarnation of his dead love, Hohner is determined to prevent her from singing the Marcellina role.

With Susanna Foster.

While examining her throat in his laboratory, the physician hypnotizes her into believing she can never sing again. Hoping to free her of Hohner's evil powers, Angela's fiance, Franz (Turhan Bey), reaches the King (Scotty Beckett) who orders Angela to give a command performance. During Franz's absence, the crazed Hohner makes an attempt on her life, but the physician's housekeeper (Gale Sondergaard) intervenes and accuses him of Marcellina's murder. As Angela sings *The Magic Voice*, Hohner tries to stop her by mental telepathy, but the powers of Franz's love triumphs. Escaping into a subterranean room containing the body of Marcellina, the doctor accidentally disturbs a lighted bowl. Soon, he and Marcellina are consumed in a fiery holocaust.

NOTES

In Karloff's first color film, producer–director George Waggner hoped to duplicate his previous

With Turhan Bey and Susanna Foster.

success of *Phantom of the Opera*. He united him with its star Susanna Foster and used the same *Phantom* stage which was originally constructed for the 1925 Lon Chaney version.

Waggner chose to remake the early Jean Hersholt starrer *The Climax,* released in 1930. This talkie version was expanded from the old, popular 1909 Edward Locke five-character play in which the villain was a secondary character. Much revived, it was one of the earliest plays to deal with mental telepathy. In the early talkie, the villain was played by actor LeRoy Mason. For the 1944 remake, the role and plot was enlarged to create an elaborate costume vehicle for Karloff and the

With Ludwig Stossel.

The destruction of the secret burial chamber.

Technicolor camera. The locale was also shifted from Italy to a mythical European country.

To display Susanna Foster's vocal gifts, the music for the operettas were adapted from Chopin and Shubert themes by Edward Ward. Its lyrics were written by Director Waggner.

REVIEW

. . . The Climax starts off on a fine ghoulish tangent, but soon wanders off the straight, narrow and creepy path onto a sidetrack of conventional boy–girl doings . . . with Karloff turned more than a little ridiculous among a group of harmless music lovers whose member includes a boy King.

George Waggner, the director, knows a thing or two about the color camera. For Karloff's flashback memories he uses a circle in clear focus in the center of the screen, surrounded by blurred, varicolored light . . .

. . . The Climax has too much difficulty deciding whether to keep its mind on music or murder.

New York Herald Tribune

Discussing a scene with June Vincent and Producer–Director George Waggner.

181

House of Frankenstein

Universal   1944.

CREDITS

Directed by Erle C. Kenton. *Screenplay by* Edward T. Lowe. *Based on a story by* Curt Siodmak. *Photography,* George Robinson. *Editor,* Philip Cahn. *Musical score,* Hans J. Salter. *Makeup,* Jack Pierce. Released December 1944. Running time: 70 minutes.

CAST

Boris Karloff, Lon Chaney Jr., John Carradine, J. Carroll Naish, Lionel Atwill, George Zucco, Anne Gwynne, Peter Coe, Elena Verdugo, Glenn Strange, Sig Ruman, William Edmunds, Charles Miller, Philip Van Zandt, George Lynn, Michael Mark, Frank Reicher, Brandon Hurst, Olaf Hytten and Joe Kirk.

SYNOPSIS

Imprisoned for fifteen years because of gruesome experiments, Dr. Gustav Niemann (Boris Karloff) escapes from Neustadt Prison. He is accompanied by Daniel (J. Carroll Naish), a psychopathic hunchback killer. After joining Prof. Lampini's (George Zucco) traveling Chamber of Horrors, they murder Lampini. Impersonating the showman, Niemann seeks revenge against the men responsible for his imprisonment. Reaching Reigelburg, Niemann restores one of the exhibits, Count Dracula (John Carradine), to life. Dracula murders the Burgomaster (Sig Ruman) and nearly kills his granddaughter (Anne Gwynne). Abandoned by Niemann, he is destroyed by the first rays of daylight. Arriving in Frankenstein,

With John Carradine

Daniel gives shelter to an abandoned gypsy girl (Elena Verdugo). Searching for Frankenstein's diary, they discover the frozen bodies of the Frankenstein Monster (Glenn Strange) and the Wolf Man (Lon Chaney Jr.) beneath the ruins of the Frankenstein castle.

After the entire group returns to Niemann's old laboratory, the doctor murders two old enemies and removes their still–alive brains, intending to place them into the skulls of the Wolf Man and the Monster. But the Wolf Man is killed by the gypsy with a silver bullet after attacking her. Blaming Niemann for her death, Daniel strangles the doctor, but the revitalized Monster murders

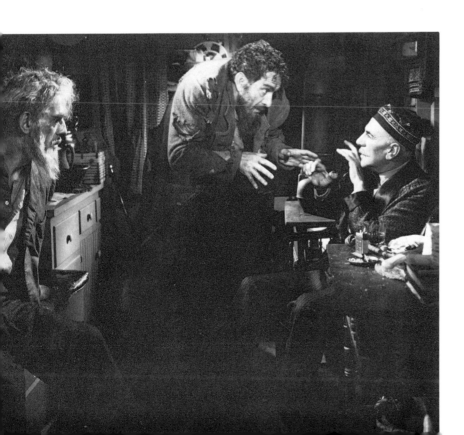

With J. Carroll Naish and George Zucco.

183

With J. Carroll Naish.

the hunchback. Attracted to the laboratory, a mob of villagers pursue the Monster and Niemann into a nearby body of quicksand where they both slowly sink out of sight.

NOTES

A sequel to *Frankenstein Meets the Wolf Man* which was released the year before, *House of Frankenstein* boasted a cast which included the Frankenstein Monster, the Wolf Man and Dracula together for the first time. At one point, during the film's preshooting stages, the writers intended to include another one of Universal's family of Monsters, the Mummy, into the script, but the idea was eliminated at the last minute.

During the filming, Karloff coached his successor, Glenn Strange, in the role of the Frankenstein Monster. Strange was so adept in the role,

With Glenn Strange and
J. Carroll Naish.

184

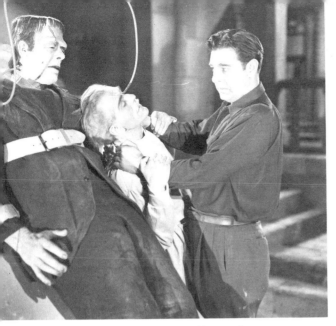

With Glenn Strange and Lon Chaney Jr.

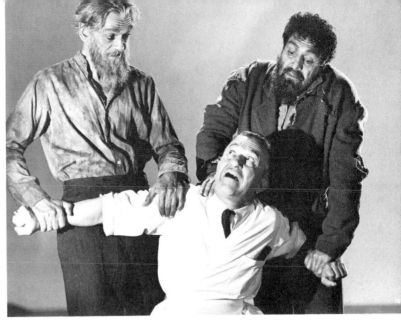

Clowning on the set with Jack Pierce and J. Carroll Naish.

he repeated it in the remainder of the series, *House of Dracula* (1945) and *Abbott and Costello Meet Frankenstein* (1948).

In *House of Frankenstein,* Karloff appeared as the brother of a former assistant to the original Dr. Frankenstein. This was his last appearance in the Frankenstein series produced by Universal.

REVIEW

Frankenstein's Monster, Dracula, and the Wolf Man provide three-ply horror display in this chiller-diller meller. Aimed entirely for suspense and weird dramatics, picture is a solid entry for the attention of the Horror addicts and will click for good biz. . . .

Karloff is the usual menace in lead role of the scientist, with Naish particularly well cast as the hunchback. Lon Chaney Jr. is the Wolf Man, while John Carradine steps into the Dracula assignment. Erle Kenton generates plenty of creeps and suspense in the direction, while script has all the ingredients required of a horror show.

"Walt," *Variety*

With Glenn Strange.

The Bodysnatcher

RKO Radio   1945.

CREDITS

Directed by Robert Wise. *Produced by* Val Lewton. *Screenplay by* Philip MacDonald *and* Carlos Keith (Val Lewton). *Based on the short story by* Robert Louis Stevenson. *Photography,* Robert de Grasse. *Editor,* J. R. Whittredge. *Musical score,* Roy Webb. Released March 1945. Running time: 77 minutes.

CAST

Boris Karloff, Bela Lugosi, Henry Daniell, Edith Atwater, Russell Wade, Rita Corday, Sharyn Moffett, Donna Lee, Bill Williams, Robert Clarke and Jim Moran.

SYNOPSIS

By 1832, Edinburgh's indignation against grave-robbers who supplied the medical profession with "subjects" finally quiets down. One who escaped retribution was Dr. MacFarlane (Henry Daniell), head of a medical school. His past was concealed

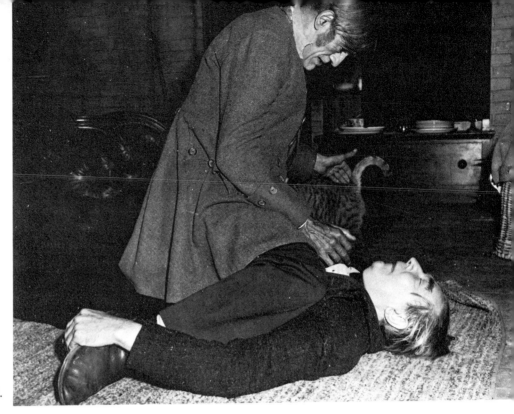

With Bela Lugosi.

by the silence of his assistant, Gray (Boris Karloff), who secretly gloats in the influence he flaunts over MacFarlane. Fettes (Russell Wade), a young medical student, is shocked to learn that Gray, under the guise of a cab driver, supplies stolen bodies to the doctor. After learning MacFarlane cannot cure Georgina (Sharyn Moffett), a paralyzed child, because of the unavailability of "subjects," Gray turns up with the freshly murdered corpse of a young street singer. MacFarlane

operates on Georgina, but the child is still unable to walk.

MacFarlane's servant, Joseph (Bela Lugosi), learns of the street singer's murder and tries to blackmail the cab driver. Gray cold-bloodedly murders Joseph and delivers the body to the doctor, who discovers it in a brine vat. Determined to be rid of Gray for good, MacFarlane finally kills him and dissects the body. Learning his operation on Georgina is a success after all, the doctor

With Russell Wade (seated) and Henry Daniell.

187

persuades Fettes to help him obtain a "subject" for further experiments. Leaving the cemetery with the body of a woman, MacFarlane imagines it to be Gray and becomes hysterical. His carriage goes off a cliff, killing him.

NOTES

In Karloff's first film with the RKO Val Lewton unit, he and Bela Lugosi were given top billing for box-office purposes. But Henry Daniell was really the star of the film, with Karloff in the major supporting role. Ironically, Lugosi's role was a minor (but effective) one and his last association with Karloff.

REVIEWS

Skillfully produced and directed, this horror melodrama should more than satisfy those who like

With Russell Wade.

With Russell Wade and Bela Lugosi.

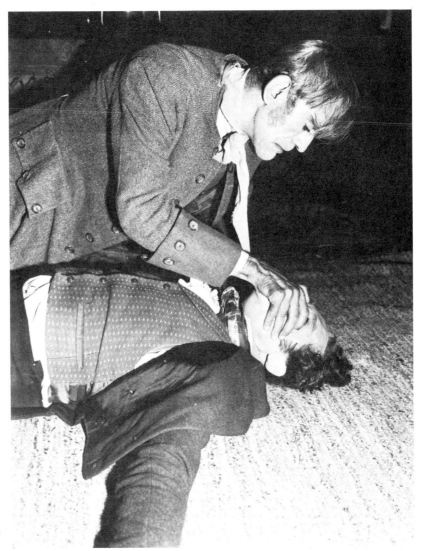

With Henry Daniell.

their screen entertainment weird and spine-chilling . . . Boris Karloff, as the blackmailing grave-robber, gives one of the best performances of his career, while Henry Daniell is not far behind him . . . their ghoulish, maniacal doings keep one on the edge of his seat. . . .

Harrison's Reports

Like all Val Lewton productions, *The Body-snatcher* shows a humane sincerity and a devotion to good cinema . . . however, much of the picture is more literary than lively and neglects its crass possibilities as melodrama . . . the last passage in the picture is as all-out, hair-raising a climax to a horror film as you are ever likely to see.

Time

Val Lewton, who has a way with weird and occult tales, has found one to his liking by an old master . . . and produced it with all the modern staging and lighting effects which have won him and the horror picture a considerable following. . . .

Karloff gives an excellent portrayal of the evil cabby and Daniell almost matches him as the harassed doctor. . . .

Motion Picture Herald

189

BURIED, ALIVE!

A beautiful girl on a desolate isle...where a monster that was once a man...deals out terrifying tortures!

BORIS KARLOFF in ISLE of the DEAD

with ELLEN DREW
MARC CRAMER

Re released by
R K O
RADIO
PICTURES

Produced by VAL LEWTON · Directed by MARK ROBSON · Written by Ardel Wray

Isle of the Dead

RKO Radio   1945.

CREDITS

Directed by Mark Robson. *Screenplay by* Ardel Wray, Josef Mischel *and* Val Lewton. *Photography,* Jack MacKenzie. *Editor,* Lyle Boyer. Released September 1945. Running time: 72 minutes.

CAST

Boris Karloff, Ellen Drew, Marc Cramer, Katherine Emery, Helene Thimig, Alan Napier, Jason Robards Sr., Ernst Dorian, Skelton Knaggs and Sherry Hall.

SYNOPSIS

During the Balkan War of 1912, General Pherides (Boris Karloff) rows to a tiny Grecian island to visit the grave of his wife. Oliver Davis (Marc Cramer), an American newspaperman, accompanies him. After finding the coffin looted by thieves, they accept lodging in the household of Albrecht (Jason Robards Sr.), an antique collector. But they soon discover plague has infested the island. One by one, members of the household die of the dread disease. But Kyra (Helene Thimig), superstitious old crone, believes Thea

With Helene Thimig, Ellen Drew and Katherine Emery.

(Ellen Drew), an attractive Greek girl, is responsible for the deaths because she is a vampire.

Soon one of the members (Katherine Emery) succumbs to a cataleptic trance. Believing her to be dead, the rest entomb her in a coffin. But that night she recovers and rises from her tomb. Unhinged by the plague and Kyra's superstitions, the general attempts to kill Thea, but the cataleptic slays the crazed general in the nick of time and falls to her death from a steep cliff.

With Marc Cramer.

192

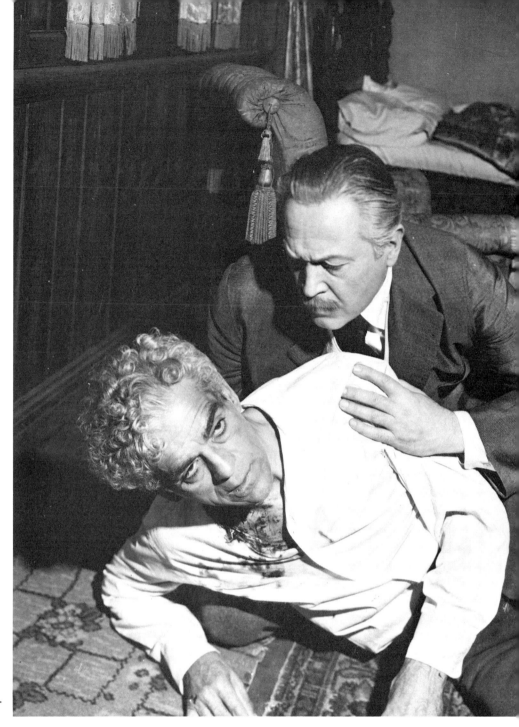

With Jason Robards Sr.

NOTES

The story line of *Isle of the Dead* was supposedly suggested by the famed, atmospheric painting by Swiss Romanticist Arnold Boecklin. Filming was interrupted on two occasions: Suffering from an old back injury, Karloff was rushed to the hospital for an emergency spinal operation; Actress Rose Hobart was replaced in the role of the cataleptic (Mrs. St. Aubyn) by Katherine Emery.

REVIEW

. . . A slow conversation piece. . . . It's been better handled and directed than most of the so–called "horror" films, though thriller fans will find its lack of action a drag and its suspense only mildly interesting. Even Boris Karloff fans will note the tired way he rambles through it all.

Some good sets, acting and moody atmosphere give the yarn a better backing than it deserves. Karloff . . . is more paternal than menacing. . . .

"Bron," *Variety*

With Joan Newton.

Bedlam

RKO Radio   1946.

CREDITS

Directed by Mark Robson. *Screenplay by* Mark Robson *and* Carlos Keith (Val Lewton). *Suggested by the* William Hogarth Engraving Plate No. 8, *The Rake's Progress. Photography,* Nicholas Musuraca. *Editor,* Lyle Boyer. Released May 10, 1946. Running time: 80 minutes.

CAST

Boris Karloff, Anna Lee, Billy House, Richard Fraser, Glenn Vernon, Ian Wolfe, Jason Robards Sr., Leland Hodgson, Joan Newton, Elizabeth Russell, Skelton Knaggs and Robert Clarke.

SYNOPSIS

In the London of 1761, Bedlam was under the cruel domination of its chief warden, Master Sims (Boris Karloff). One example of his callousness is charging citizens tuppence apiece to watch the antics of the lunatics. During a special performance for Lord Mortimer (Billy House) and his

With Richard Fraser and Anna Lee.

aristocratic friends, one of the lunatics (Glenn Vernon) smothers to death because he is gilded, an idea used later in the James Bond film, *Goldfinger*. Nell Bowen (Anna Lee), mistress of Lord Mortimer, is shocked at Sims' mistreatment of his charges and humiliates him publicly. After she turns against her benefactor and tries to seek reforms at the institution, Sims has her committed to Bedlam on false charges.

With the moral support of a friendly Quaker (Richard Fraser), she wins the inmates over by kindness and understanding. Learning her friends have succeeded in granting her a new trial, Sims attempts to unhinge her mentally. But the inmates turn against the warden, making him their prisoner. After placing him on trial for his life, Sims is stabbed to death by one of the inmates. Panic-stricken, they wall up his body in masonry. With

With Ted Billings (holding cross) and Anna Lee.

With Robert Clarke (Right).

Sims' mysterious disappearance, Bedlam is transformed into a humane institution.

NOTES

In spite of *Bedlam*'s being the most expensive of Lewton's films, the studio was short–sighted as to the film's qualities and did not give it the distribution it deserved. The film ended Karloff's association with Lewton, who hoped to make further "specials." Because the horror–film cycle petered

With Glenn Vernon.

196

On the set with Director Mark Robson and Producer Val Lewton.

out during this postwar period, *Bedlam* was Karloff's last serious effort in horror melodrama until the fifties.

The standing church set from *Bells of St. Mary's* was used for the notorious asylum. Hogarth's paintings were also used throughout the film as a transitional device. Inevitably, these were usually deleted from television prints.

REVIEWS

... An elaborate improvisation, but not an improvement, on one of Hogarth's paintings ... I am afraid that this particular film is a careful, pretty failure, and I regret and somewhat fear Lewton's recent interest in costume movies, which seem to draw on his romantic–literary weaknesses more than on his best abilities, which are poetic and cinematic. But Lewton ... would have to make much less sincere and pleasing films than this before I would review them disrespectfully.

James Agee, *The Nation*

... Producer Val Lewton and writer–director Mark Robson wring some effective moments of pity and horror out of the assorted lunatics and ... attack the more callous self–delusions of the Age of Reason.... But sincere, artful and scary as the best of *Bedlam* is, its horror and high–mindedness don't always blend smoothly.

Time

The Secret Life of Walter Mitty

RKO Radio   1947.

CREDITS

Directed by Norman Z. McLeod. *Produced by* Samuel Goldwyn. *Screenplay by* Ken Englund *and* Everett Freeman. *Based on the short story by* James Thurber. *Photography,* Lee Garmes. *Editor,* Monica Collingswood. *Color by* Technicolor. Released September 1, 1947. Running time: 110 minutes.

CAST

Danny Kaye, Virginia Mayo, Boris Karloff, Fay Bainter, Ann Rutherford, Thurston Hall, Gordon Jones, Florence Bates, Konstantine Shayne, Reginald Denny, Henry Corden, Doris Lloyd, Fritz Feld, Frank Reicher, Milton Parsons and the Goldwyn Girls.

SYNOPSIS

Walter Mitty (Danny Kaye), a mild–mannered proofreader for a pulp magazine publishing house, escapes periodically from his routine existence in daydreams. A young woman, Rosalind van Hoorn (Virginia Mayo), enlists his aid in escaping from a strange character who is following her. Soon, Mitty becomes involved with an international ring of jewel thieves who are scheming to steal an incredible fortune in gems from her uncle (Konstantine Shayne). While trying to help her, members of the gang make attempts on Mitty's life, including a phony psychiatrist, Dr. Hollingshead (Boris Karloff), who tries to push him out of a window. After Rosalind falls into their clutches, Mitty rescues her and captures the entire ring following a series of wild, slapstick chases.

With Milton Parsons, Konstantine Shayne and Henry Corden.

With Thurston Hall, Fay Bainter and Danny Kaye.

REVIEW

With the nation's box offices aching at this particular moment for a smash comedy, Samuel Goldwyn has stepped in with exactly the right prescription. . . .

Some of the . . . Thurber fans may squeal at the pic, since there's been considerable change from the famed short story . . . Karloff wins heftiest yaks in a scene in which he plays a phony psychiatrist convincing Mitty he's nuts.

Norman Z. McLeod's direction keeps the action relatively fast and sharp. Production in general is up to the usual top Goldwyn standard.

"Herb," *Variety*

With Virginia Mayo.

Lured

United Artists   1947.

CREDITS

Directed by Douglas Sirk. *Screenplay by* Leo Rosten. *Photography,* William Daniels. *Editor,* John M. Foley. Released September 1947. Running time: 102 minutes.

CAST

George Sanders, Lucille Ball, Charles Coburn, Alan Mowbray, Sir Cedric Hardwicke, George Zucco, Joseph Calleia, Tanis Chandler and Boris Karloff.

SYNOPSIS

In London, young women mysteriously disappear after answering attractively phrased advertisements in the daily newspapers. Scotland Yard persuades Sandra Carpenter (Lucille Ball), an American dance–hall hostess, to lure the intellectual, but demented killer into the open by answering these advertisements. While answering these ads, she encounters an odd collection of crackpots and eccentrics, including a suspicious suspect. But this turns out to be a mentally unhinged, but

With Lucille Ball.

harmless dress designer (Boris Karloff). Eventually, Sandra uncovers a gang of white slavers headed by Dr. Moryani (Joseph Calleia), whom Scotland Yard believe to be responsible for the murders.

But circumstantial evidence convicts Sandra's fiance, nightclub proprietor Robert Fleming (George Sanders), of the murders. Knowing Fleming is innocent, Sandra risks her life in a harrowing climax, revealing her fiance's partner (Sir Cedric Hardwicke) to be the actual murderer.

NOTES

Lured is a remake of the French film *Pièges* (1939) directed by Robert Siodmak. It starred Erich von Stroheim and Maurice Chevalier. Karloff's role was originally played by von Stroheim in the French version.

REVIEW

Handsome roster of players plus an equally handsome production should make this pic a positive factor at the b. o. *Lured* misses entry into the jackpot class because of its familiar . . . scripting job.

. . . Lucille Ball meets up with a demented courtier played in broad style by Boris Karloff. Sequence, an effective goose–pimpler in itself, is entirely irrelevant to the central action, and Karloff's stay . . . is limited to little more than five minutes. . . .

"Herm," *Variety*

With Howard Da Silva and Robert Warwick

Unconquered

Paramount   1947.

CREDITS

Directed by Cecil B. DeMille. *Produced by* Cecil B. DeMille. *Screenplay by* Charles Bennett, Frederick M. Frank *and* Jesse Lasky Jr. *Based on the novel by* Neil H. Swanson. *Photography,* Ray Rennahan. *Editor,* Anne Bauchens. *Makeup,* Wally Westmore. *Color by* Technicolor. Released September 24, 1947. Running time: 146 minutes.

CAST

Gary Cooper, Paulette Goddard, Howard Da Silva, Boris Karloff, Cecil Kellaway, Ward Bond, Katherine DeMille, Henry Wilcoxon, Sir C. Aubrey Smith, Victor Varconi, Virginia Grey, Porter Hall, Mike Mazurki, Richard Gaines, Virginia Campbell, Gavin Muir, Alan Napier, Nan Sunderland, Marc Lawrence, Jane Nigh, Robert Warwick, Lloyd Bridges, Raymond Hatton, Chief Thundercloud, Jack Pennick, Lex Barker and Charles Middleton.

SYNOPSIS

In 1763 in colonial America, Martin Garth (Howard Da Silva), a powerful trader, tries to protect his interests by secretly trading guns to the Indians to stop the westward movement of settlers. Garth attempts to purchase young Abby Hale (Paulette Goddard), a British indentured servant, for himself, but Virginia patriot, Capt. Christopher Holden (Gary Cooper), outbids the trader and then frees her. Hoping to push the white man back to the sea for good, Garth encourages an Indian rebellion on Fort Pitt led by Chief Guyasuta (Boris Karloff). Jealous of Abby, Garth's wife, Hannah (Katherine DeMille), arranges to have the young woman captured by the Indians.

Holden rescues Abby in the nick of time from a slow, torturous death at the hands of Guyasuta. As the pair return to the safety of Fort Pitt, they find it already besieged by Indians. Using his resourcefulness, Holden saves Fort Pitt and its occu-

With Gary Cooper and Marc Lawrence.

pants from the Indians by obtaining reinforcements. After killing Garth in the fort's stable, Holden is finally reunited with Abby for good.

REVIEW

... The movie is ... to be sure, a huge ... colored chunk of hokum; but the most old-fashioned thing about it is its exuberance ... which ... Director DeMille preserves almost single-handed from the old days. ...

Mixed with all the nineteenth-century theatricalism, the early twentieth-century talent for making movies move, and the overall impression of utter falsity, *Unconquered* has some authentic flavor of the period.

Time

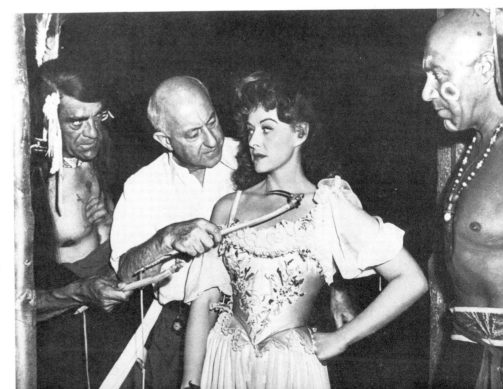

Rehearsing a scene with Director Cecil B. DeMille and Paulette Goddard.

With Ralph Byrd and Anne Gwynne.

Dick Tracy Meets Gruesome

RKO Radio   1947.

CREDITS

Directed by John Rawlins. *Screenplay by* Robertson White *and* Eric Taylor. *Based on the cartoon strip* Dick Tracy *by* Chester Gould. *Photography,* Frank Redman. *Editor,* Elmo Williams. Released November 12, 1947. Running time: 65 minutes.

CAST

Boris Karloff, Ralph Byrd, Anne Gwynne, Edward Ashley, June Clayworth, Lyle Latell, Tony Barrett, Skelton Knaggs, Jim Nolan, Joseph Crehan, Milton Parsons and Lex Barker.

SYNOPSIS

A mysterious gas which temporarily paralyzes people falls into the possession of a disreputable doctor, L. E. Thal (Edward Ashley). Realizing the tremendous criminal possibilities of the strange gas, Gruesome (Boris Karloff), an ex-convict, enlists Thal's aid to stage a daring bank robbery. But Tess Truehart (Anne Gwynne) witnesses the robbery and calls Dick Tracy (Ralph Byrd) who is soon hot on their trail. After wrecking their getaway car, Gruesome escapes, but his accomplice (Tony Barrett) is taken to a hospital.

With Lyle Latell.

Learning that Dr. Thal intends to give himself up, the criminal cold–bloodedly kills him. After informing the newspapers that Gruesome's accomplice will squeal, Tracy sets a trap by impersonating him in the hospital bed. The killer takes the bait and kidnaps Tracy back to his hideout.

Tracy's plan almost backfires when his aide Pat Patton (Lyle Latell) loses the trail. But the criminal is finally apprehended by the famous detective.

REVIEW

. . . *Dick Tracy Meets Gruesome* is a chiller–diller

With Tony Barrett.

With Edward Ashley and
Skelton Knaggs.

With Ralph Byrd and Harry Strang.

. . . given an added asset . . . that Boris Karloff heads the cast.

Yarn casts Karloff as Gruesome, stalking through his familiar menacing scenes, pet stunt being to put his victims in a huge furnace for safekeeping. To give it a . . . poetic justice twist, story has Karloff escaping a familiar fiery death only by last–second intervention by Tracy. . . .

Karloff, per usual, thefts every scene in which he appears. Byrd is acceptable as Tracy, even to resemblance to the square–jawed detective. . . .

Director . . . Rawlins employs almost serial–type action . . . with surprisingly good results. . . .

"Wear," *Variety*

206

With Susan Hayward and Russell Simpson.

Tap Roots

Universal–International   1948.

CREDITS

Directed by George Marshall. *Screenplay by* Alan LeMay. *Based on the novel by* James Street. *Photography,* Lionel Lindon *and* Winton C. Hoch. *Editor,* Milton Carruth. *Makeup,* Bud Westmore. *Color by* Technicolor. Released August 1948. Running time: 109 minutes.

CAST

Van Heflin, Susan Hayward, Boris Karloff, Julie London, Whitfield Connor, Ward Bond, Richard Long, Arthur Shields, Griff Barnett, Sondra Rogers, Ruby Dandridge and Russell Simpson.

SYNOPSIS

At the outbreak of the Civil War, Lebanon Valley attempts to secede from the state of Mississippi and remain neutral. Hating slavery, its leader, Hoab Dabney (Ward Bond), and a faithful Indian friend of the family, Tishomingo (Boris Karloff), promise to protect the valley against the Confederate army. Hoping to win Hoab's headstrong daughter, Morna (Susan Hayward), Keith Alexander (Van Heflin) a notorious newspaper publisher, joins Dabney. Morna's plans to marry Clay MacIvor (Whitfield Connor), a Confederate officer, are postponed, following a riding accident. Unknown to Morna, Clay loves her sister, Aven (Julie London), and suddenly elopes with her. Keith persists in trying to win Morna's affections, but she rebuffs him.

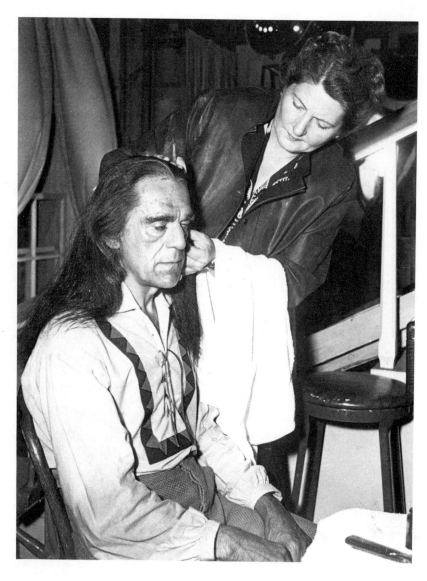

Being made up for the role of
Tishomingo.

Soon Clay becomes a major in the Confederate
army. Learning he intends to destroy Hoab's in-
surrection, Morna spends the night with him, hoping to delay his forces. But the soldiers annihilate
the defenders. Keith and Clay finally have a
showdown in a swamp, and the officer is killed.
After the Confederate army leaves the valley,
Keith is finally reunited with Morna.

REVIEW

. . . *Tap Roots* . . . never reaches epic proportions,
is too long, and not always put together smoothly.

However, the plot's high romance . . . color lensing of the Civil War costumes, sex implications
and plot action are salable values . . .

. . . Characters are colorful, if unbelievable, and
are generally well played, with few exceptions.

. . . Karloff is excellent as an Indian friend of
the family. . . . .

Smoky Mountains location in North Carolina
and Tennessee, where the Mississippi story was
filmed, lends itself magnificently to the color lensing. . . .

"Brog," *Variety*

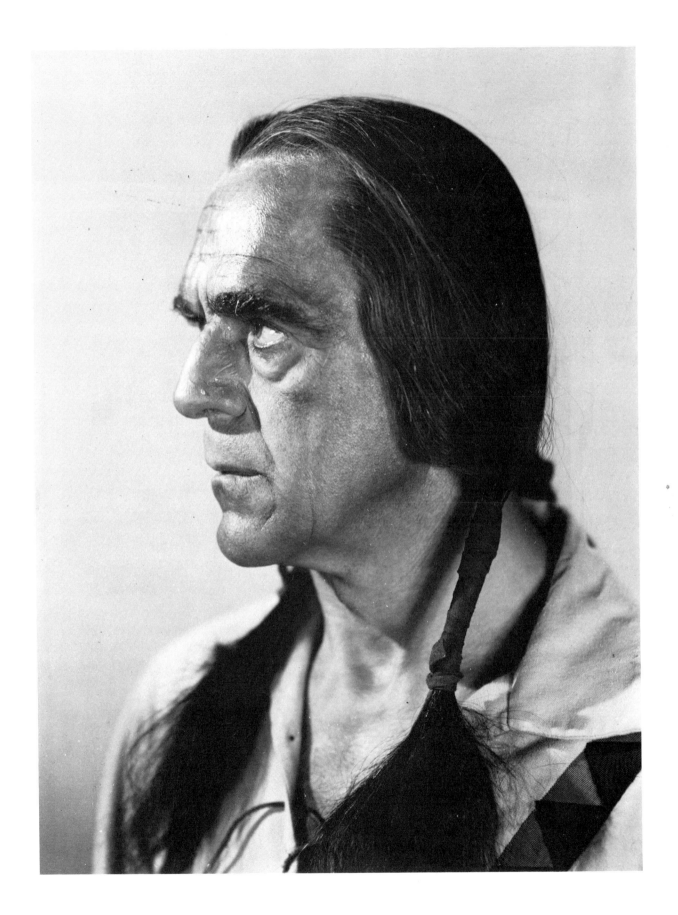

Abbott and Costello
Meet the Killer, Boris Karloff

Universal–International   1949.

CREDITS

Directed by Charles T. Barton. *Screenplay by* Hugh Wedlock Jr., Howard Snyder *and* John Grant. *Photography,* Charles Van Enger. *Editor,* Edward Curtiss. Released August 1949. Running time: 84 minutes.

CAST

Bud Abbott, Lou Costello, Boris Karloff, Lenore Aubert, Gar Moore, Donna Martell, Alan Mowbray, James Flavin, Roland Winters, Nicholas Joy, Mikel Conrad, Morgan Farley, Victoria Horne, Percy Helton and Claire Dubrey.

SYNOPSIS

A famous attorney is murdered at the Lost Caverns Hotel. Circumstantial evidence points to Freddie Phillips (Lou Costello), a bellhop. His pal, Casey Edwards (Bud Abbott), is the house detective. He tries to help Freddie, but succeeds only in getting him into worse trouble. Several more murders occur, casting further suspicion on the bellhop. Hoping to conceal their shady pasts, the hotel guests scheme to let Freddie take the blame for the murders. Swami Talpur (Boris Karloff), their leader, tries to hypnotize Freddie into signing a false confession, and then killing himself. But the bellhop's subnormal mentality prevents this.

Intending to use Freddie as bait to catch the real murderer, Inspector Wellman (James Flavin) announces the bellhop possesses a clue to the murderer's identity. That night, Freddie is lured to the Lost Caverns. There, he is nearly killed by a mysterious assailant. Returning to the hotel, Freddie finally exposes the murderer.

NOTES

Encouraged by the box–office success of *Abbott and Costello Meet Frankenstein* of the year before, Universal decided to team their former horror star, Karloff, with the studio's top comics. Though the script contained a "red herring" role for the actor, the vehicle enjoyed the distinction as possibly being one of the few films containing the name of its star in the title. More important, the publicity gimmick revealed the (still potent) box–office strength of the actor's name.

Because the length of the title inconvenienced the limitations of the exhibitor's marquees, the title was later shortened to *Abbott and Costello Meet the Killer*. The film's success paved the way for the comics to co–star with other assorted "monsters" and villains in a series of further spoofs.

REVIEW

Well lubricated with double–takes, gags and familiar slapstick, this is an entry that qualifies easily as escapist film fare. . . . The plot is just one of those things. But the dialog is buttered so well with the bon mots and pratfalls which have made the comedians an American institution that their fans will likely overlook the inanities of the "story."

Boris Karloff is amusing as a swami whose hypnotic powers are frequently ineffective. . . . Direction of Charles T. Barton is competent. . . .

"Gilb," *Variety*

With Lou Costello and Bud Abbott.

With Harry Hayden, Roland Winters, Claire Dubrey, Victoria Horne and James Flavin.

211

The Strange Door

Universal–International   1951.

CREDITS

Directed by Joseph Pevney. *Screenplay by* Jerry Sackheim. *Based on the story* The Sire de Maletroit's Door *by* Robert Louis Stevenson. *Photography,* Irving Glassberg. *Editor,* Edward Curtiss. Released December 1951. Running time: 81 minutes.

CAST

Charles Laughton, Boris Karloff, Sally Forrest, Richard Stapley, Michael Pate, Paul Cavanagh, Alan Napier, William Cottrell, Morgan Farley, Edwin Parker and Charles Horvath.

With William Cottrell and Charles
Laughton.

SYNOPSIS

In eighteenth–century France, a nobleman, Alan de Maletroit (Charles Laughton), is deserted by a woman who marries his brother, Edmond (Paul Cavanagh), instead. After she dies in childbirth, the crazed nobleman imprisons his brother. The daughter of the union, Blanche (Sally Forrest), raised by her uncle Alan, is unaware that her father is a prisoner beneath the chateau. After Blanche comes of age, de Maletroit intends to complete his revenge by marrying his niece to

Denis de Beaulieu (Richard Stapley), an irresponsible wastrel. The nobleman successfully lures the young man to his chateau after framing him for murder. Contrary to de Maletroit's plans, they fall in love.

After forcing the couple to marry, de Maletroit imprisons them in the same dungeon with his brother, intending to crush them to death. But Voltan (Boris Karloff), a faithful servant, destroys the mad nobleman and rescues the prisoners in the nick of time.

With Paul Cavanagh.

213

With Charles Laughton.

REVIEW

The horror theme has been revived . . . in *The Strange Door*. There are good elements of suspense and characterization in this celluloid adaptation of a Robert Louis Stevenson story.

As the master fiend, Laughton is well cast. He revels in his lines and leers at his victims almost to the point of overplaying. Karloff competently portrays the loyal servant. . . .

"Gilb," *Variety*

With Richard Stapley.

214

The Black Castle

Universal–International   1952.

CREDITS

Directed by Nathan Juran. *Screenplay by* Jerry Sackheim. *Photography,* Irving Glassberg. *Editor,* Russell Schoengarth. *Musical score,* Joseph Gershenson. Released December 1952. Running time: 81 minutes.

CAST

Richard Greene, Boris Karloff, Stephen McNally, Paula Corday, Lon Chaney Jr., John Hoyt, Michael Pate, Nancy Valentine, Tudor Owen, Henry Corden and Otto Waldis.

SYNOPSIS

Sir Ronald Burton (Richard Greene), an eighteenth–century English adventurer, believes his two friends have been murdered by Count von Bruno (Stephen McNally) on his Black Forest estate. Arriving at von Bruno's castle to accumulate evidence, Burton learns von Bruno's unhappy wife, Elga (Paula Corday), and Dr. Meissen (Boris Karloff), the castle physician, are virtual prisoners. Suspecting Burton's motives, von Bruno and Gargon (Lon Chaney Jr.), a giant, mute, scarred henchman, discover the Englishman was

With Paula Corday and Richard Greene.

responsible for their being captured and tortured by African natives for ivory poaching. The count schemes to have Burton killed in a leopard hunt, but he escapes.

Burton leaves to present proof of von Bruno's guilt to the Austrian authorities. But he returns after learning the count intends to slay Elga be-cause she loves the Englishman. While trying to rescue Elga, Burton kicks Gargon to his death in an alligator pit. After Burton is imprisoned with Elga, von Bruno plans to bury them alive. To help them, Dr. Meissen secretly gives the prisoners a drug giving them a temporary appearance of death. But von Bruno discovers this plan and

With Michael Pate, Stephen McNally and Richard Greene.

With Stephen McNally and Paula Corday.

kills the doctor. Before von Bruno seals their coffins, he is killed by dueling pistols placed in Burton's hands by Dr. Meissen.

REVIEW

. . . The chiller antics are in line with the period programmers turned out by Universal some seasons back and are played straight by the good cast.

. . . Marquee strength . . . enters into the spirit of things with plenty of acceptable scenery–chewing that brings off the meller antics neatly.

. . . Low–key lensing . . . is . . . done excellently in a scene showing a black leopard that highlights the chiller sequences. . . .

"Brog," *Variety*

With Paula Corday and Richard Greene.

Abbott and Costello
Meet Dr. Jekyll and Mr. Hyde

Universal–International   1953.

CREDITS

Directed by Charles Lamont. *Screenplay by* Lee Loeb *and* John Grant. *Photography,* George Robinson. *Editor,* Russell Schoengarth. *Makeup,* Bud Westmore *and* Jack Kevan. Released August 1953. Running time: 77 minutes.

CAST

Bud Abbott, Lou Costello, Boris Karloff, Helen Westcott, Craig Stevens, Reginald Denny, John Dierkes and Edwin Parker.

SYNOPSIS

During the turn of the century, two American police officers, Slim (Bud Abbott) and Tubby (Lou Costello), study London police methods. While breaking up a suffragette demonstration, they meet Vicky Edwards (Helen Westcott), a musical hall performer. Her guardian, Dr. Henry Jekyll (Boris Karloff), is secretly experimenting with transplanting character traits and personalities in humans and animals. With the aid of a hypodermic injection, Dr. Jekyll transforms himself into a half–man–half–beast, Mr. Hyde, a monstrous creature who is terrorizing London. Desiring Vicky for himself, Jekyll becomes Mr. Hyde and attempts to murder her fiance, Bruce Adams

With Helen Westcott.

With Bud Abbott and Lou Costello.

(Craig Stevens), at a music hall. By sheer luck, Tubby captures the monster, but it reverts to Dr. Jekyll. After the authorities refuse to believe he is the monster, Jekyll is released.

While Slim and Tubby hunt for the monster in Dr. Jekyll's home, Tubby accidentally falls on a hypodermic and becomes a monster also. Later, Hyde abducts Vicky and is pursued back to Jekyll's home. But Bruce rescues her from his clutches as the monster falls to his death from an upstairs window. Tubby eventually reverts to his normal self after biting several policemen who also turn into monsters.

NOTES

Karloff returned to playing a monster for the first time in fourteen years since *Son of Frankenstein* in the famed Robert Louis Stevenson story. But it was a mixed blessing for his fans as the classic tale of a split personality was formularized to fit the talents of the comedy team. For his dual role as Mr. Hyde, Karloff wore a rubber mask and was substituted for by a stuntman (Eddie Parker) in the more athletic scenes. It was the seventh in the *Abbott and Costello Meet* series and Karloff's last film for Universal, the studio where he achieved his fame.

The series concluded with *Abbott and Costello Meet the Mummy* in 1955.

REVIEW

Buffoonery and bestiality join hands when Abbott and Costello trade slapstick pranks with that hellion of the film world, Boris Karloff, in this latest adventure. The net result of this combination provides some pleasing nonsense and horror.

A & C fans should enjoy the proceedings, but pure horror enthusiasts may be a trifle disappointed, as the horror is played mostly for laughs. Karloff slinks and growls as the animal Mr. Hyde and is most suave as the good doctor. . . .

Motion Picture Herald

With Bud Abbott and Lou Costello.

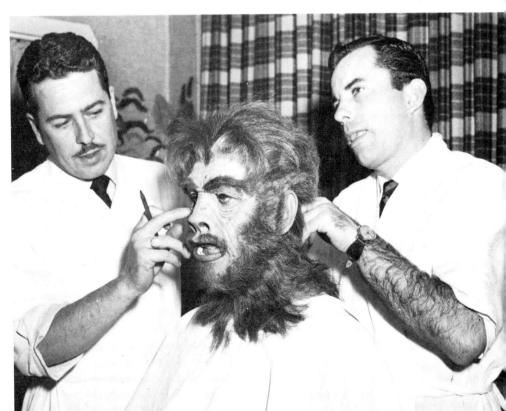

Makeup men Jack Kevan and Bud Westmore transform Karloff into Mr. Hyde.

With Patrizia Remiddi.

Monster of the Island

Romana Films   1953.

CREDITS

Directed by Roberto Montero. *Screenplay by* Roberto Montero *and* Alberto Vecchietti. *Based on a story by* Alberto Vecchietti. *Photography,* Augusto Tiezzi. *Editor,* Iolanda Benvenuti. Released 1953. Running time: 87 minutes.

CAST

Boris Karloff, Franco Marzi, Renata Vicario, Patrizia Remiddi, Iole Fierro, Carlo Duse, Germana Paolieri, Giuseppe Chinnici, Giulio Battiferri, Domenico De Ninno, Clara Gamberini and Salvatore Scibetta.

SYNOPSIS

Authorities in Rome are alarmed at the growing traffic of narcotics on the island of Ischia. Andreani (Franco Marzi), a government agent, is assigned to unmask the identity of the ringleader and destroy the smuggling ring. Working undercover, Andreani meets Gloria (Renata Vicario),

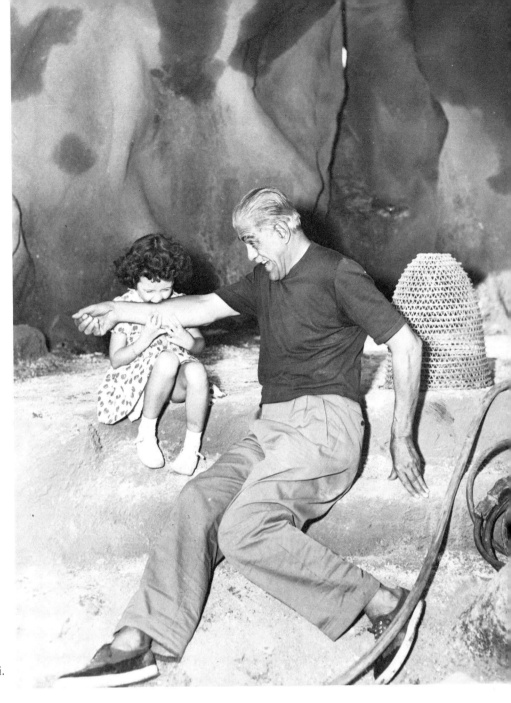

On the set with Patrizia Remiddi.

a local singer, and learns she is familiar with members of the gang. The agent is also befriended by Don Gaetano (Boris Karloff), an elderly philanthropist, who continues to finance a nursery he founded. Unexpectedly, the smugglers kidnap Andreani's child (Patrizia Remiddi), threatening to murder her if the agent's investigation continues.

With the aid of Gloria, he locates the smuggler's hideout. But he is captured and learns his friend, Don Gaetano, is the head of the ring. Aware that the police are closing in, Gaetano uses Andreani's child as a hostage in order to escape.

But the agent overpowers the ringleader and rescues her. After every member of the ring is rounded up by the police, Andreani and his family return to the mainland.

NOTES

Monster of the Island was filmed in Paolis Studios in Rome and on the island of Ischia (near Napoli). It was released under the title *Il Mostro Dell' Isola* in Italy and finally reached the United States four years later, but played only Italian–language theatres.

With Lou Krugman and Nino Marcel.

The Hindu

United Artists   1953.

CREDITS

Directed by Frank Ferrin. *Screenplay by* Frank Ferrin. *Photography,* Allen Stensvold *and* Jack McCoskey. *Editor,* Jack Foley. *Color by* Eastman Color. Released 1953. Running time: 81 minutes.

CAST

Boris Karloff, Nino Marcel, Lou Krugman, Reginald Denny, Victory Jory, June Foray, Lisa Howard, Jay Novello, Peter Coe, Paul Marion, Vito Scotti, Lou Merrill, Larry Dobkin and Jeanne Bates.

SYNOPSIS

An evil cult of fire–worshippers terrorizes native villages in India. After his family is killed in a forest fire started by the cult, Gunga Ram (Nino Marcel), a fearless elephant trainer, swears vengeance. The young mahout seeks aid from his friend, the Maharajah of Bakore (Lou Krugman), and his aide, General Pollegar (Boris Karloff). But they refuse to believe in the cult's existence. Ram captures the high priestess (June Foray) of the cult and one of her followers, but they are released after they convince the Maharajah they are merely entertainers.

Ram finally locates the secret hiding place of the cult deep in the jungle. There, he discovers the high priestess and her cult executing weird

As General Pollegar.

rites before a large, unholy idol. The mahout is captured and sentenced to be burned alive. But his two jungle pets—an elephant and a tiger—rescue him and destroy the priestess. With the destruction of the cult and their idol, Ram finally avenges his family's death.

NOTES

The film was made on location in the southern Indian state of Mysore by radio producer Frank Ferrin. The plot was obviously inspired by the U.S. television series with Nino Marcel the elephant boy. Karloff's scenes were obviously added to give the film exhibitor appeal. After giving it scanty distribution upon its original release,

United Artists withdrew the film from circulation and released it two years later, retitled *Sabaka*.

REVIEW

. . . This is a rather amateurish program adventure melodrama that may get by with the youngsters and uncritical adults . . . it is actionful . . . the scenes of wild animals stampeding through a forest fire are impressive. The proceedings . . . are not easy to follow, and most of the time one is in doubt as to what is going on . . . Karloff, Denny and . . . Jory are the only members of the cast . . . known to American audiences, but their roles are . . . brief, even though they are starred . . . color photography is only fair . . . much of it is fuzzy.
Harrison's Reports

With Beverly Tyler.

Voodoo Island

United Artists   1957.

CREDITS

Directed by Reginald LeBorg. *Screenplay by* Richard Landau. *Photography,* William Margulies. *Editor,* John F. Schreyer. Released February 1957. Running time: 77 minutes.

CAST

Boris Karloff, Beverly Tyler, Murvyn Vye, Elisha Cook, Rhodes Reason, Jean Engstrom, Frederich Ledebur, Glenn Dixon, Owen Cunningham, Herbert Patterson and Jerome Frank.

SYNOPSIS

Phillip Knight (Boris Karloff), a professional debunker of hoaxes, is hired by a hotel builder to investigate a tropical island overrun with voodoo. A previous expedition had mysteriously disappeared. After Knight and members of his expedition arrive on the island, strange and unnatural incidents happen. But Knight continues to disbelieve in the supernatural.

As the expedition moves further into the jungle, one of them becomes a zombie (Murvyn Vye),

226

and another (Jean Engstrom) falls victim to a flesh-devouring plant. After the remainder of the group falls into the hands of a superstitious tribe of natives, Knight promises to leave the tribe in peace if the expedition is released. As the group leave the island, Knight is forced to new conclusions regarding the supernatural.

REVIEW

Carnivorous plants and zombies supply the chief menace for the principals in *Voodoo Island* . . .

. . . There's no attempt at explaining how various mysterious things happen in the . . . script . . . but the thriller gimmicks come off with Reginald LeBorg's direction.

. . . Aubrey Schenck–Howard W. Koch production was lensed on Kauai Island, Hawaii, so backgrounds have a helpful freshness as the characters are put through plot perils. Karloff doesn't have to exert himself much to handle his standard character. . . . None of the performances is more than stock.

"Brog," *Variety*

With Murvyn Vye.

With Rhodes Reason, Murvyn Vye, Elisha Cook, Jean Engstrom and Beverly Tyler.

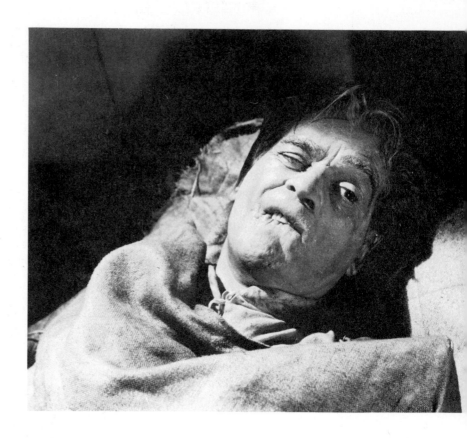

The Haunted Strangler

Metro–Goldwyn–Mayer   1958.

CREDITS

Directed by Robert Day. *Screenplay by* Jan Read *and* John C. Cooper. *Photography,* Lionel Banes. *Editor,* Peter Mayhew. Released June 1958. Running time: 78 minutes.

CAST

Boris Karloff, Anthony Dawson, Jean Kent, Elizabeth Allan, Derek Birch, Dorothy Gordon, Diane Aubrey, Tim Turner, Vera Day, Max Brimmell, Leslie Perrins, John Fabian, Desmond Roberts and Jessica Cairns.

SYNOPSIS

In 1860, a suspect labeled the "Haymarket Strangler" is convicted of strangling and slashing five young women to death. Twenty years after the execution in London's Newgate Prison, James Rankin (Boris Karloff), a criminologist, suspects the authorities hanged the wrong man. While trying to solve the mystery, Rankin discovers the missing murder weapon, a scalpel, in the convicted man's coffin. While holding the instrument in his hand, he has a maniacal fit and murders a music hall singer (Jean Kent). He has a mental blackout the following day and is unable to remember his crime.

His wife (Elizabeth Allan) reveals he is the "Haymarket Strangler" of twenty years ago, and

With Elizabeth Allan.

that she helped him escape from a mental institution when he experienced amnesia. With the scalpel in his hand again, Rankin transforms into his Hyde–like self and murders his wife. Finally committed to an asylum, he murders a guard and escapes. Rankin is finally slain by the police while trying to replace the scalpel in the coffin of the "Strangler."

REVIEWS

Makes for mild horror. . . . There are, to say the least, interesting touches, full–blooded scenes and a cute little rat who nibbles contentedly at a rather handsome skull . . . Karloff masters both characters and comes off well in each. . . . Technically, production is worthy, especially considering its budget.

"Ron," *Variety*

For all its attempts to invoke Gothic atmosphere, film has little more life than a chestful of old Victorian costumes. Blame it on the lack of real spirit in the screenplay . . . or on the flat direction. . . . Seldom manages to free itself from synthetic posturing. The same goes for Karloff.

The New York Times

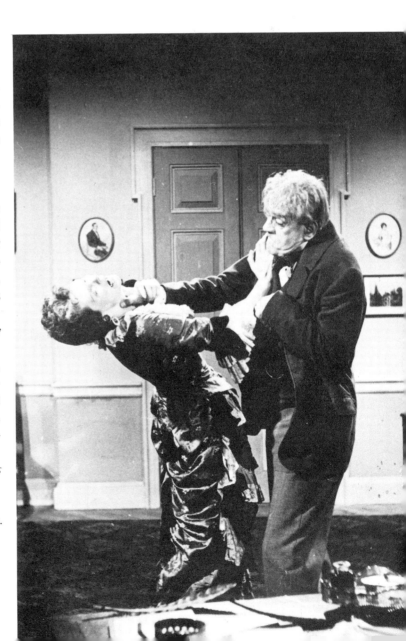

With Elizabeth Allan.

With Norbert Schiller and
Jana Lund.

Frankenstein 1970

Allied Artists   1958.

CREDITS

Directed by Howard Koch. *Screenplay by* Richard
Landau *and* George Worthing Yates. *Based on a
story by* Aubrey Schenck *and* Charles A. Moses.
Photography, Carl E. Guthrie. *Editor,* John A.
Bushelman. *Makeup,* Gordon Bau. Released July
6, 1958. Running time: 83 minutes.

CAST

Boris Karloff, Tom Duggan, Jana Lund, Donald
Barry, Charlotte Austin, Irwin Berke, Rudolph
Anders, John Dennis, Norbert Schiller and Mike
Lane.

SYNOPSIS

His body scarred by his Nazi captors during
World War II, Baron Victor von Frankenstein
(Boris Karloff) plans to recreate the legendary
Monster originally conceived by his ancestor. In
order to raise money to purchase an atomic reac-
tor to complete his experiments, he permits an
American television unit to film a show at his
German castle. His servant, Shuter (Norbert
Schiller), accidentally discovers von Franken-
stein's hidden laboratory. After giving him a post-
hypnotic suggestion of obedience, the baron kills
Shuter and transfers his brain into the Monster's

skull. After the arrival of the reactor, von Frankenstein instills his creation with life, but the Monster is sightless.

After two members of the television unit are mysteriously murdered, the baron's old friend, Wilhelm Gottfried (Rudolph Anders), suspects the truth. He also becomes the baron's next victim; his eyes are placed into the Monster's skull to give him sight. Soon, the feminine star (Jana Lund) of the troupe is lured into the clutches of the Monster. But its brain suddenly reverts to normal and it attacks von Frankenstein instead. As they struggle in the laboratory, atomic steam is unleashed, destroying the Monster and its creator.

NOTES

During the late fifties, television exposure of Karloff's old Frankenstein films and the Hammer Film color remakes helped spark a new horror cycle in Hollywood. Among the many new low–budget shockers, two films inspired by Mary Shelley's famous character appeared: *I Was a Teenage Frankenstein* and *Frankenstein's Daughter*. Allied

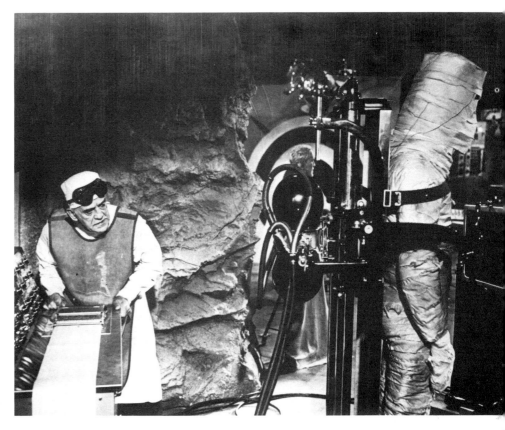

With Mike Lane.

Artists decided to modernize the story and injected a bit more size into their budget than usual. To add prestige to *Frankenstein 1970,* they signed Karloff for the starring role. Lacking the necessary facilities, the film was shot in Cinemascope in the Warner Bros. studios.

REVIEW

Well–made entry in the horror class . . . Karloff, made up to look rather like a disfigured Hindenburg, does a careful, convincing job with his role, which is competently written. . . . The professionalism of the cast is somewhat thrown by the appearance in important roles of Tom Duggan and Irwin Berke, local TV personalities, who do well enough but are hardly in a class with Karloff. . . . Camera work is fluid and perceptive. . . . Sets are a major asset in believability. . . . Title, incidentally, means nothing.

"Powe," *Variety*

On the set with Director Howard Koch.

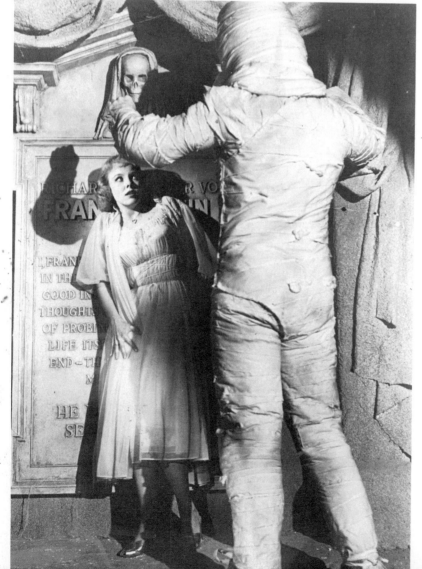

Jana Lund and Mike Lane.

With Walter Miller

Days of Thrills and Laughter

20th Century–Fox   1961.

CREDITS

Produced and written by Robert Youngson. *Narrated by* Jay Jackson. *Sound effects,* Alfred Dahlem *and* Ralph F. Curtiss. Released March 1961. Running time: 93 minutes.

CAST

Douglas Fairbanks, Charlie Chaplin, Stan Laurel, Oliver Hardy, Houdini, Pearl White, Harry Langdon, Ben Turpin, Charlie Chase, Snub Pollard, Mack Sennett, Fatty Arbuckle, Mabel Normand, Ford Sterling, Boris Karloff, Warner Oland, Ruth Roland, Monty Banks, Al St. John, Cameo the Wonder Dog, Keystone Cops and The Sennett Bathing Beauties.

NOTES

In this third of Youngson's silent film compilations, Karloff appeared in a brief clip from the 1929 Mascot serial, *King of the Kongo.*

With Walter Miller (wearing white shirt).

REVIEW

. . . The thrillers, however, emerge just as funny as the comedies, thanks to the sophistication of retrospect. . . . The sound effects seem to take something away from the original charm rather than adding to it . . . as a cross–section of the early cinema, *Days of Thrills and Laughter* is an enchanting glimpse of a more frenetic, light–hearted . . . world than the one we live in now.

Variety

With Peter Lorre, Vincent Price,
Hazel Court and Olive Sturgess.

The Raven

American International   1963.

CREDITS

Directed by Roger Corman. *Screenplay by* Richard Matheson. *Based on the poem by* Edgar Allan Poe. *Photography,* Floyd Crosby. *Editor,* Ronald Sinclair. *Makeup,* Ted Coodley. *Color by* Pathécolor. Released February 1963. Running time: 86 minutes.

CAST

Vincent Price, Peter Lorre, Boris Karloff, Hazel Court, Olive Sturgess, Jack Nicholson, Connie Wallace, William Baskin and Aaron Saxon.

SYNOPSIS

Believing his wife Lenore (Hazel Court) to be dead, a sixteenth–century magician, Dr. Erasmus Craven (Vincent Price), goes into retirement. One night, he is visited by a talking raven requesting help. Erasmus discovers it is fellow magician, Dr. Bedlo (Peter Lorre), transformed into a bird by the master sorcerer, Dr. Scarabus (Boris Karloff), as punishment for challenging his powers. After restoring Dr. Bedlo to his human form, Craven learns a woman resembling Lenore has been observed at Scarabus's castle. Craven joins forces with Bedlo in his plans for revenge. Unknown to Craven, these developments are a plan by Dr. Scarabus to lure Craven to his castle to extract more power in the magical arts from him.

Arriving at Scarabus' castle, Craven learns

235

With Vincent Price.

With Vincent Price.

With Peter Lorre and Vincent Price.

that Lenore pretended to be dead in order to become the sorcerer's mistress and to share his wealth and influence. Suddenly Scarabus imprisons the magicians and threatens to torture Craven's daughter unless he reveals the secrets of his magical powers. In a fit of temper, Scarabus changes Bedlo back into a raven again. The bird cuts Craven's bonds, enabling him to combat Scarabus in a fantastic duel of magic. Craven defeats his rival and turns the castle into a fiery holocaust.

NOTES

Stimulated by the success of *Tales of Terror* (1962), American International decided to unite its two stars, Peter Lorre and Vincent Price, together with Karloff in another Edgar Allan Poe adaptation. After a four–year absence from the screen, the veteran actor and his co–stars were ballyhooed as the "Triumvirate of Terror" in the studio's fifth color film based on Poe. Photographed in Panavision, *The Raven* was shot in three weeks and was the most expensive Poe film ($350,000) to date.

REVIEW

Edgar Allan Poe might turn over in his grave at this nonsensical adaptation of his immortal poem, but audiences will find the spooky goings–on a cornpop of considerable comedic dimensions. . . . Special effects figure prominently to add sometimes spectacular interest when the two hurl their talents at each other . . . Les Baxter's . . . score is another assist in adding an eerie touch. Characterizations are played straight for . . . comedy value sparked by . . . ridiculous lines . . . Price makes his theatricalism pay off. Karloff plays it smooth. Lorre is almost cute. . . .

Variety

237

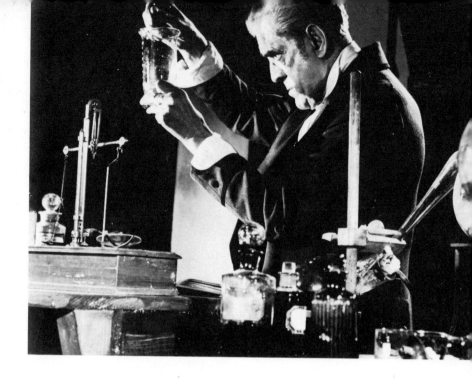

Corridors of Blood

CREDITS

Directed by Robert Day. *Screenplay by* Jean Scott
Rogers. *Photography,* Geoffrey Faithfull. *Editor,*
Peter Mayhew. Released April 1963. Running
time: 85 minutes.

CAST

Boris Karloff, Betta St. John, Francis Matthews,
Francis De Wolff, Adrienne Corri, Frank Pettin-
gell, Finlay Currie, Christopher Lee, Marian
Spencer, Carl Bernard, Charles Lloyd Pack,
Yvonne Warren, Robert Raglan, Basil Dignam,
John Gabriel, Nigel Green and Howard Lang.

SYNOPSIS

Before the discovery of anesthesia, operations in
London hospitals were screaming bloody nightmares. In 1840, Dr. Bolton (Boris Karloff), a
humanitarian surgeon, attempts to eliminate all
the pain and suffering connected with surgery.
While experimenting on himself, Bolton becomes
addicted to drugs. During a hospital demonstration of his pain–killing gas, his patient revives and
attacks the attending physicians and students. Dismissed from his post, the disgraced surgeon is
unable to continue his experiments because he has
been denied access to the ingredients.

Under the influence of drugs, Bolton wanders
into the Seven Dials, a disreputable tavern. Soon,
the surgeon is under the evil influence of the inn-
keeper, Black Ben (Francis De Wolff), and his
cohort, Resurrection Joe (Christopher Lee). Intending to sell cadavers to hospitals, they supply
Bolton with drugs in exchange for his signature
on bogus death certificates. After the criminals
murder a hospital guard, the police round up the
gang. In a struggle, the doctor is killed. Bolton's
son, Jonathan (Francis Matthews), continues his
father's work until anesthesia becomes a reality.

NOTES

Corridors of Blood was produced by John Croy-
don at MGM's studio in England five years

With Francis Matthews (Center).

prior to its American release. Originally titled *Doctor from Seven Dials,* the film was shot back–to–back with *The Haunted Strangler* by the same director, Robert Day.

REVIEW

Rather surprisingly, the first quarter of *Corridors of Blood* is pretty good. For a while it suggests those gaslit melodramas of Old London. . . . Horror they had, also a serious underlying purpose-fulness. . . . This portion is forthright, picaresque and carries ugly conviction, and Mr. Karloff is a persuasive, if lamblike protagonist. Then the film turns into a plodding, shuddersome exercise in blood and pain. It's the old one–two, strictly for the sake of shock.

Howard Thompson, *The New York Times*

With Christopher Lee.

With Christopher Lee, Adrienne Corri and Francis De Wolff.

239

With Jack Nicholson.

The Terror

American International   1963.

CREDITS

Directed by Roger Corman. *Screenplay by* Leo Gordon *and* Jack Hill. *Photography,* John Nicholaus. *Editor,* Stuart O'Brien. *Color by* Pathécolor. Released September 1963. Running time: 81 minutes.

CAST

Boris Karloff, Jack Nicholson, Sandra Knight, Richard Miller, Dorothy Neumann and Jonathan Haze.

SYNOPSIS

Andre Duvalier (Jack Nicholson), an officer of Napoleon's army, is lost somewhere on the Baltic coast. Collapsing from exhaustion, he is awakened by a young woman (Sandra Knight) who leads him to fresh water. Andre is drawn to her as in a trance, but she disappears. The officer is restored to health in the hovel of a strange old woman (Dorothy Neumann) and her mute servant. Duvalier learns that the mysterious young woman can be found in the castle of Baron von Leppe (Boris Karloff). He discovers the baron to be an elderly recluse, brooding over the loss of his long–dead wife. Andre recognizes the strange girl's likeness in a painting which von Leppe insists is a portrait of his dead wife.

Later, Andre learns the old woman is really a witch, using the girl as an instrument of revenge to drive the baron to suicide. He murdered her son, Erik, twenty years ago because he loved the baron's wife. Completely mad, the baron decides to drown himself and the girl by letting the sea into the subterranean cellars of the castle. As von

240

With Basil Rathbone, Vincent Price and Peter Lorre.

Comedy of Terrors

American International   1963.

CREDITS

Directed by Jacques Tourneur. *Screenplay by* Richard Matheson. *Photography,* Floyd Crosby. *Editor,* Anthony Carras. *Makeup,* Carlie Taylor. *Color by* Pathécolor. Released December 1963. Running time: 88 minutes.

CAST

Vincent Price, Peter Lorre, Boris Karloff, Basil Rathbone, Joe E. Brown, Joyce Jameson, Beverly Hills, Paul Barsolow, Linda Rogers, Luree Nicholson, Buddy Mason and Rhubarb the Cat.

SYNOPSIS

During the 1890s, a New England funeral establishment is troubled with financial and domestic difficulties. Its owner, Waldo Trumbull (Vincent Price), has let the business run down because of his alcoholism and indolence. Trumbull practices his undertaking profession only when a financial crisis erupts. This he does by inventing "customers" with the aid of his ex–criminal assistant, Felix Gillie (Peter Lorre). Amaryllis (Joyce Jameson), Trumbull's neglected wife, is aggravated by her drunken husband who threatens to murder her father, Amos Hinchley (Boris Karloff), with poison. The senile founder of the establishment believes it to be medicine. Unknown to Trumbull, Felix and Amaryllis fall in love.

Faced with paying their back rent, they decide to wipe out their debt and obtain an extravagant funeral by securing their landlord, John F. Black (Basil Rathbone), as their "customer." Following several unsuccessful attempts on the landlord's life, Black supposedly dies. But the landlord rises from his family vault, full of revenge. After the two undertakers are chased around their house by the axe–wielding Black, Trumbull finally kills him with a bullet. During a struggle with Felix, Trumbull is knocked unconscious. Believing his son–in–law ill, Amos Hinchley administers the deadly "medicine" to him. With Trumbull dead, Amaryllis and Felix are now free to begin their new life together.

NOTES

Comedy of Terrors was shot in twenty days on a twelve–hour day shooting schedule. Director Tourneur utilized the graveyard set from *The Premature Burial* (1962).

REVIEW

. . . Sends a bunch of horror and mystery actors off on a childish spree which may be giving them a lot of fun but does nothing for their audience.

Boris Karloff is on hand to add his own touches to the act but he has limited opportunities as a doddering, deaf, old fool.

The story is one of the thinnest ever to find its way to a movie screen.

Alton Cook, *New York World-Telegram*

On the set with daughter Sara Jane.

With Joyce Jameson and Vincent Price.

Black Sabbath

American International   1964.

CREDITS

Directed by Mario Bava. *Screenplay by* Marcello Fondato, Alberto Bevilacqua *and* Mario Bava. *Based on stories by* Anton Chekhov, Howard Snyder *and* Alexei Tolstoy. *Photography,* Ubaldo Terzano. *Editor,* Mario Serandrei. *Color by* Pathécolor. Released May 1964. Running time: 99 minutes.

THE DROP OF WATER

CAST

Jacqueline Pierreux and Milly Monti.

THE TELEPHONE

CAST

Michele Mercier and Lidia Alfonsi.

245

THE WURDALAK

CAST

Boris Karloff, Susy Andersen, Mark Damon, Glauco Onorato, Rika Dialina and Massimo Righi.

SYNOPSIS

Nurse Helen Corey (Jacqueline Pierreux) is called to the home of ailing clairvoyant, Madame Perkins. Arriving there, she discovers the old recluse is dead. Filled with greed, Helen removes a diamond ring from the corpse and wears it on the way home. Later that night, she is plagued by the mysterious dripping of water and the ghostly phantom of Madame Perkins. The next day, the police discover Helen's dead body; her finger is discolored, as though a ring had been torn from it.

Rosy (Michele Mercier), an attractive call girl,

With Glauco Onorato and Massimo Righi.

is terrorized by strange telephone calls threatening her life. Panic–stricken, Rosy calls her girl friend, Mary, who agrees to stay overnight with her. Rosy learns the caller is the man she betrayed and sent to prison. Later that night, the escaped convict enters the apartment and mistakenly strangles Mary. Terrified, Rosy stabs him to death. But the phone mysteriously rings again; the dead man informs her he will torment her forever and ever.

Traveling through Eastern Europe, Vladimir D'Urfe (Mark Damon), a young nobleman, encounters a family fearfully awaiting the return of their father, Gorca (Boris Karloff). He had gone away to kill Alibek the bandit, but had warned them if he should fail to return in five days, he would have become a Wurdalak or vampire: creatures who thirst for the blood they love most dearly. As the nobleman waits with them, he falls in love with young Sdenka (Susy Andersen). On the fifth day Gorca returns, bearing the severed head of Alibek. To their horror, Gorca has become a Wurdalak. Vladimir and Sdenka flee to an old convent after Gorca kills every member of the family, turning them into vampires also. Gorca finally tracks down Sdenka and kills her. Having become a Wurdalak, she kills Vladimir as he embraces her. The Wurdalak cycle finally reaches its awful climax.

NOTES

In this Italian–French–American coproduction, Karloff introduced the three episodes and appeared in the last and longest segment, *The Wurdalak*, a Tolstoy adaptation.

REVIEW

The Wurdalak, longest and scariest episode . . . represents that hoary old horror, Boris Karloff, as an East European vampire. . . . Silly stuff, of course, but it's nice to know that a monster emeritus can somehow manage to eeeeeeeek out a living.

Time

With Rika Dialina.

On the set with Jim Nicholson and Keenan Wynn.

Bikini Beach

American International   1964.

CREDITS

Directed by William Asher. *Screenplay by* William Asher, Leo Townsend *and* Robert Dillon. *Photography,* Floyd Crosby. *Editor,* Fred Feitshans. *Color by* Pathécolor. Released July 1964. Running time: 100 minutes.

CAST

Frankie Avalon, Annette Funicello, Martha Hyer, Don Rickles, Harvey Lembeck, Keenan Wynn, John Ashley, Jody McCrea, Candy Johnson, Danielle Aubry, Meredith MacRae, Delores Wells, Paul Smith, James Westerfield, Donna Loren, Janos Prohaska, Timothy Carey, Val Warren, Little Stevie Wonder, The Pyramids and The Exciters.

SYNOPSIS

Frankie (Frankie Avalon), Dee Dee (Annette Funicello) and their surfing gang arrive at Bikini Beach for another vacation of surfing, dancing and music. To their dismay, they discover Harvey Huntington Honeywagon (Keenan Wynn) plans to secure the beach to construct a senior citizen's retirement community. Eric Von Zipper (Harvey Lembeck) and his motorcycle gang also invade the area and enthusiastically joins Honeywagon's campaign against the kids.

A British recording star, The Potato Bug (Frankie Avalon), threatens to steal Dee Dee away from Frankie. But Frankie defeats The Potato Bug and Von Zipper at a drag race and the motorcycle gang run for their lives. Influenced by the surfing gang's schoolteacher (Martha Hyer), Honeywagon ceases his campaign against the kids as Frankie and Dee Dee are reunited.

NOTES

Karloff made an unbilled brief appearance as the "Art Dealer" who observes the teenagers scrapping and remarks, "Monsters!" This was the third of the successful "beach" series produced by American International.

REVIEW

... First–rate satire is so overloaded with coatings of slapstick that the satire will be lost on the ... mass of youngsters. ... There's some excellent writing ... which even spoofs the cyclist's adoration of the Hitler myth ... Asher's nimble direction never lets anything slow the pace he knows is necessary to this type of film. ...

Variety

With Suzan Farmer and
Nick Adams.

Die, Monster, Die

American International   1965.

CREDITS

Directed by Daniel Haller. *Screenplay by* Jerry Sohl. *Based on the story* The Color Out of Space by H. P. Lovecraft. *Photography,* Paul Beeson. *Editor,* Alfred Cox. *Makeup,* Jimmy Evans. *Color by* Colorscope. Released October 1965. Running time: 80 minutes.

CAST

Boris Karloff, Nick Adams, Freda Jackson, Suzan Farmer, Terence DeMarney, Patrick Magee, Paul Farrell, George Moon, Gretchen Franklin, Sydney Bromley and Billy Milton.

SYNOPSIS

American scientist Stephen Reinhart (Nick Adams) arrives in Arkham, a remote English village, to visit his fiancee, Susan Witley (Suzan Farmer), and her parents. Her crippled father, Nahum Witley (Boris Karloff), tries to discourage him from seeing his daughter, but Stephen is finally reunited with Susan. Later, her bedridden mother (Freda Jackson) pleads with him to take Susan away. Stephen notices her face is covered with a heavy, black veil. After Witley's manservant (Terence DeMarney) dies mysteriously, Stephen is convinced a strange manner of evil has stricken the house and its occupants.

Susan's mother has become a hideously, disfigured mutant who attempts to attack Stephen and Susan, but suddenly disintegrates into a mound of black ashes. Soon Stephen discovers the grim truth: the occupants of the house are slowly deteriorating into horrible monsters due to radioactivity from a fallen meteorite. Realizing his mistake in experimenting with the monster–stone, Witley tries to destroy it. But he is transformed

As a disintegrating mutant.

into a glowing mutant himself. His reason gone, Witley tries to kill the lovers, but he crashes to the bottom of a staircase and disintegrates instead. As the house becomes a holocaust, Susan and Stephen escape to safety.

REVIEW

If the purpose of a horror film is to scare people, then American International's latest nightmare . . . meets its obligations completely. Some of the most frightening faces to appear on the screen have been employed to produce the necessary "chilling" effect in *Die, Monster, Die*.

. . . And what's a horror film without Boris Karloff, that master of subtle terror whose talents have not diminished over the years? He's in top form in *Die, Monster, Die*. . . .

There really isn't anything original about *Die, Monster, Die*, but all the elements necessary to make a good tale of terror can be found in the film. . . .

Motion Picture Herald

With Suzan Farmer.

With Susan Hart.

Ghost in the Invisible Bikini

American International   1966.

CREDITS

Directed by Don Weis. *Screenplay by* Louis M. Heyward *and* Elwood Ullman. *Photography,* Stanley Cortez. *Editors,* Fred Feitshans *and* Eve Newman. *Makeup,* Ted Coodley. *Color by* Pathécolor. Released April 6, 1966. Running time: 82 minutes.

CAST

Tommy Kirk, Deborah Walley, Aron Kincaid, Quinn O'Hara, Jesse White, Harvey Lembeck, Nancy Sinatra, Basil Rathbone, Patsy Kelly, Boris Karloff, Susan Hart, Claudia Martin, Francis X. Bushman, Benny Rubin, Bobbi Shaw, George Barrows, Luree Holmes, Alberta Nelson, Andy Romano and The Bobby Fuller Four.

SYNOPSIS

In the depths of his deserted mansion, the corpse

of Hiram Stokley (Boris Karloff) receives a heavenly visitor, his long–dead sweetheart, Cecily (Susan Hart). Hiram learns he can become young again and enter the pearly gates if he performs a good deed within twenty–four hours. Upstairs, young Chuck Phillips (Tommy Kirk) and the other heirs assemble for the reading of Stokley's will at midnight. Unknown to them, Reginald Ripper (Basil Rathbone), executor of the estate, schemes to eliminate the others in order to keep the money for himself. He is aided by his evil daughter, Sinistra (Quinn O'Hara), and others.

Soon, Eric Von Zipper's (Harvey Lembeck) motorcycle gang gets mixed up in his plans also, and everyone is brought together in Stokley's secret "chamber of horrors" beneath his mansion. Hiram and Cecily finally foil Ripper's schemes, and his wealth goes to the rightful heirs. Receiving his reward, Hiram becomes young again and enters heaven with Cecily.

NOTES

Ghost in the Invisible Bikini was the largest budgeted of the "beach" pictures. But it became a box–office failure and was the last of that genre American International produced.

REVIEW

The inane script . . . is not only tired but borrows from such other sources as the curtain line of *Some Like It Hot*. . . . This year's crop of boys isn't up to the earlier "beach" cavaliers . . . Karloff and the other veterans are only along for the ride . . . Stanley Cortez's camera . . . makes good use . . . in exploring some . . . fascinating sets evidently left over from the Poe period . . . a good try but short on script and inspiration.

"Robe," *Variety*

On the set with Francis X. Bushman and Basil Rathbone.

As "The Rat" (Left).

The Daydreamer

Embassy   1966.

CREDITS

Directed by Jules Bass. *Animation sequences staged by* Don Duga. *Screenplay by* Arthur Rankin Jr. *Based on Stories and Characters created by* Hans Christian Andersen. *"Animagic" Photography,* Tad Mochinga. *Live–action Photography,* Daniel Cavelli. *Color by* Eastman Color. Released June 1966. Running time: 101 minutes.

CAST

Paul O'Keefe, Jack Gilford, Ray Bolger and Margaret Hamilton.

Also featuring the Voices of: Cyril Ritchard, Hayley Mills, Burl Ives, Tallulah Bankhead, Terry–Thomas, Victor Borge, Ed Wynn, Robert Harter, Patty Duke, Boris Karloff, Sessue Hayakawa and Robert Goulet.

NOTES

Karloff was the menacing voice of "The Rat" in this internationally produced, live–action "Animagic" puppet fantasy.

With Robert Vaughn.

The Venetian Affair

Metro–Goldwyn–Mayer   1967.

CREDITS

Directed by Jerry Thorpe. *Screenplay by* E. Jack Neuman. *Based on the novel by* Helen MacInnes. *Photography,* Milton Krasner. *Editor,* Henry Berman. *Color by* Metrocolor. Released January 1967. Running time: 92 minutes.

CAST

Robert Vaughn, Elke Sommer, Felicia Farr, Karl Boehm, Luciana Paluzzi, Boris Karloff, Roger C. Carmel, Edward Asner, Joe De Santis, Fabrizio Mioni, Wesley Lau and Bill Weiss.

SYNOPSIS

An American diplomat shocks the world when he blows up the international peace conference in Venice, killing all the delegates, including himself.

With Wesley Lau, Edward Asner and Robert Vaughn.

Ex–CIA man, Bill Fenner (Robert Vaughn), is rehired to locate his ex–wife (Elke Sommer), who was hired by Wahl (Karl Boehm), an important enemy agent, to befriend the American diplomat. He is also assigned to secure a report written by a mysterious political scientist, Dr. Pierre Vaugiroud (Boris Karloff). The document explains the diplomat's motive for creating the explosion.

While Fenner hunts for this report, he finds himself the target of Communist agents, assassins and blackmailers. His ex–wife is murdered, also. Anxious to obtain the report himself, Wahl abducts Fenner to his secret laboratory and injects him with a drug, intending to turn him into a mindless robot. But the drug fails. To save both their lives, Vaugiroud convinces Fenner to reveal the report's whereabouts. But Fenner discovers the scientist is drugged in the same manner as the American diplomat, also under Wahl's influence.

After killing Wahl and escaping from the laboratory, Fenner races to another peace conference in time to stop Vaugiroud from causing another explosion.

REVIEW

Dreary spy meller. . . . Pacing is tedious and plotting routine. The plot boils slowly under Jerry Thorpe's casual direction. . . . Performances are practically caricature, in a few cases leading to unwanted . . . laughs. After 92 minutes the title tune pops up under the closing credits. In one of the most ludicrous insertions of a film theme outside of deliberate satire, the romantic voice of Julius LaRosa croons—after bloody murders, torture, etc.—"Our Venetian Affair is over . . ." Yecchh!

"Murf," *Variety*

With Ian Ogilvy.

The Sorcerers

Allied Artists   1967.

CREDITS

Directed by Michael Reeves. *Screenplay by* Michael Reeves. *Photography,* Stanley Long. *Editor,* David Woodward. *Color by* Eastman Color. Released June 1967. Running time: 87 minutes.

CAST

Boris Karloff, Catherine Lacey, Ian Ogilvy, Elizabeth Ercy, Victor Henry, Susan George, Dani Sheridan, Ivor Dean, Peter Fraser, Meier Tzelniker, Bill Barnsley, Martin Terry, Gerald Campion and Alf Joint.

SYNOPSIS

Professor Monserrat (Boris Karloff), a retired stage hypnotist, creates an apparatus producing hypnotic "psychedelic" light and sound. With it, he hopes to dominate another person's mind from a distance. He is aided by Estelle (Catherine Lacey), his wife and former stage assistant. Monserrat persuades Mike (Ian Ogilvy), an irresponsible young man, to take part in his experiment, offering him excitement without any penalties. The test is a success. Not only does Mike obey his mental commands from a distance, but the professor and his wife feel the same sensation he does. Monserrat intends his discovery for mankind's benefit. But his wife is weary of poverty and persuades her husband to command Mike to steal a mink coat for her.

Soon Estelle discovers she can control the youth

alone and orders him to do more and more violent things. The professor tries to stop her, but she knocks him unconscious. After Estelle orders Mike to cold–bloodedly murder two girls, Mike tries to escape the police in an automobile. Using the remainder of his will, Monserrat causes Mike's

With Catherine Lacey.

With Ian Ogilvy.

car to crash. As the young man perishes in a burning car, the professor and his wife die in the same manner.

REVIEW

A straightforward thriller slanted to "horror" addicts . . . Boris Karloff brings his familiar adroit touch to the role of an aging somewhat nutty ex–stage mesmerist . . . Reeves, a young director who also co–scripted the yarn, has done a commendable job . . . Eastman Color lensing by Stanley Long makes good use of several London locations . . . Karloff handles his role with notable professionalism. . . .

"Rich," *Variety*

257

As "Baron Von Frankenstein."

Mad Monster Party

Embassy   1967.

CREDITS

Directed by Jules Bass. *Screenplay by* Len Korobkin *and* Harvey Kurtzman. *Based on a story by* Arthur Rankin Jr. Color by Eastman Color. Released September 1967. Running time: 94 minutes.

Featuring the puppets of: The Frankenstein Monster, Dracula, The Werewolf, The Creature, Dr. Jekyll and Mr. Hyde, The Mummy and The Hunchback of Notre Dame.

With the Voices of: Boris Karloff, Ethel Ennis, Gale Garnett, Phyllis Diller and Alan Swift.

NOTES

Karloff was the voice of "Baron Von Frankenstein" in this "Animagic" puppet comic horror film.

Targets

Paramount   1968.

CREDITS

Directed by Peter Bogdanovich. *Screenplay by* Peter Bogdanovich. *Based on a story by* Polly Platt *and* Peter Bogdanovich. *Photography,* Laszlo Kovacs. *Color by* Pathécolor. Released June 1968. Running time: 90 minutes.

CAST

Boris Karloff, Tim O'Kelly, Nancy Hsueh, James Brown, Sandy Baron, Arthur Peterson, Mary Jackson, Tanya Morgan, Monty Landis, Paul Condylis, Mark Dennis, Stafford Morgan, Peter Bogdanovich, Daniel Ades, Tim Burns, Warren White and Byron Betz.

SYNOPSIS

Byron Orlok (Boris Karloff), an aging horror star, announces he is retiring from films because the daily headlines of senseless violence have turned his performances into high camp. Urged by the studio, the actor agrees to make a final personal appearance at a drive-in showing one of his films. Meanwhile, Bobby Thompson (Tim O'Kelly), a clean-cut youth, is unable to communicate with his parents and his wife. Suddenly, the gun enthusiast goes beserk and shoots his wife, mother and a nearby grocery boy. Thompson drives away from his house, taking his arsenal with him.

Soon Thompson climbs to the top of a nearby gas tank, and uses his telescopic rifle to kill passing motorists. When the police arrive, he escapes. But they pick up his trail and pursue him to a drive-in. Thompson takes a position within the screen-tower and shoots at the terrorized audience in their cars. After several people are killed or wounded, the sniper attempts to escape. Sud-

With Daniel Ades, Nancy Hsueh
and Peter Bogdanovich.

denly, Bobby is confronted by an angry Orlok who slaps his face repeatedly. Thompson meekly surrenders and is led away by the police.

NOTES

After discovering that Karloff owed him several days of work, Roger Corman assigned his former assistant, Peter Bogdanovich, to incorporate the actor and twenty minutes of footage from his 1963 film, *The Terror,* into "any kind of film you want to make." Bogdanovich, a former free–lance film critic and writer, wrote a script inspired by the 1966 Whitman sniper killings in Texas, and Corman financed it for $130,000. *Targets* was shot in twenty–five days, using Karloff in only five of them. In order to keep the cast as economical as possible, Director Bogdanovich also doubled as an actor (director–writer Sammy Michaels) in the film.

Realizing that the only good sequence in *The Terror* footage was the flood, he cut it to three minutes and used it for the opening sequence of *Targets.* Bogdanovich also included a film clip from Karloff's 1931 film, *The Criminal Code.*

After Paramount bought the film, a wave of antigun hysteria flooded the country due to the assassination of Senator Robert F. Kennedy. At first reluctant to release it, the studio finally decided to exploit the situation by releasing it as a message for gun control. But Paramount tried to avoid any possible controversy and gave the film scanty distribution. After *Targets* was reissued later, the gun–control prologue was eliminated. Its rediscovery by the critics and the public helped launch the budding directorial career of its maker, Bogdanovich.

REVIEWS

Targets is like yesterday's headlines, today's, possibly tomorrow's. This is a timely piece that cries out loud for "gun control" and should not be taken lightly even though the object lesson is slightly out of focus.

. . . Director Peter Bogdanovich ties his two

260

stories together for a unique if theatrical climax.

. . . Boris Karloff plays the part of Byron Orlok beautifully. . . . Bogdanovich gets E for effort in his initial directorial job. *Targets* is by no means a perfect picture but it will make an indelible impression if you see it.

Wanda Hale, *New York Daily News*

Targets is a modern horror film about a figure increasingly commonplace in America, the mass murderer who kills without apparent motive.

. . . it's a cinematic dynamic and shrewd first effort, though it is ultimately a glorified B film, or exploitation shocker . . .

. . . the biggest thrill being the moments when human beings are sighted between the crosshairs and die, not knowing what hit them. That is the real terror of *Targets*. . . .

Newsday

. . . Peter Bogdanovich, former writer . . . turned screenwriter–director, has made a film of much suspense and implicit violence. . . .

Although some blood and gore are shown, it is minute in comparison with most film product today . . . Director Bogdanovich conveys moments of shock, terror . . . and fear. Feats are all the more remarkable in the face of typical low–budget shortcomings. . . .

"Murf," *Variety*

Rehearsing a scene with Director Peter Bogdanovich (on bed).

The Crimson Cult

American International   1970.

CREDITS

Directed by Vernon Sewell. *Screenplay by* Mervyn Haisman *and* Henry Lincoln. *Photography,* Johnny Coquillon. *Editor,* Howard Lanning. *Color by* Eastman Color. Released May 1970. Running time: 87 minutes.

CAST

Boris Karloff, Christopher Lee, Mark Eden, Barbara Steele, Michael Gough, Rupert Davies, Virginia Wetherell, Rosemarie Reede and Derek Tansey.

SYNOPSIS

Antique dealer, Robert Manning (Mark Eden), travels to Greymarsh Lodge in search of his missing brother, Peter. There, the Manning ancestors had lived for generations. But the lodge owner, Morley (Christopher Lee), denies his brother stayed there. Suspicious, Manning decides to learn the truth. That night, the villagers of Greymarsh celebrate the burning of the Black Witch, Lavinia (Barbara Steele), who practiced witchcraft on the villagers 300 years ago. Manning learns Morley is a descendant of Lavinia. Professor Marshe

With Mark Eden.

With Virginia Wetherell and
Mark Eden.

(Boris Karloff), a local authority on witchcraft, reveals to Manning that the dying witch cursed every villager responsible for her death and that many of their descendants met violent ends. Later, the young man learns from the butler (Michael Gough) that his brother is dead. After Morley drugs Manning's drink, the young man has a strange dream in which he is attacked by the dead witch, Lavinia.

Investigating further, Manning discovers Morley is obsessed with inflicting vengeance on every descendant responsible for Lavinia's death. Manning is overpowered and forced to witness the sacrifice of Morley's niece (Virginia Wetherell). But Professor Marshe arrives in time to prevent her murder on the sacrificial altar. Suddenly, Morley sets fire to the house and escapes. Trapped on the roof, he is transformed into Lavinia as he is consumed by the flames.

NOTES

During the filming of *The Crimson Cult,* Karloff contracted a serious case of pneumonia. Most of his scenes were played in a wheelchair and totaled eight days of shooting.

The location sequences were shot at Grimsdyke House (once the home of Sir William Sullivan of Gilbert and Sullivan fame) in Middlesex, England.

REVIEW

. . . I should be hard–pressed to defend *The Crimson Cult* on any grounds other than affection for the subject and for some of the cast . . .

. . . Karloff . . . acts with a quiet lucidity of such great beauty that it is a refreshment merely to hear him speak old claptrap. Nothing else in *The Crimson Cult* comes close to him. . . .

Roger Greenspun, *The New York Times*

Discussing a scene with Director Vernon Sewell (Left) and Christopher Lee.

With Julissa.

The Snake People

Columbia   1971.

CREDITS

Directed by Jack Hill *and* Juan Ibanez. *Screenplay by* Jack Hill. *Photography,* Austin McKinney *and* Raul Dominguez. *Color by* Eastman Color. Released March 1971. Running time: 90 minutes.

CAST

Boris Karloff, Julissa, Carlos East, Rafael Bertrand, Santanon, Quinton Bulnes and Tongolele.

SYNOPSIS

The natives of Coaibai Island are terrorized by an evil snake cult. The natives are sacrificed to the poison of a snake in the possession of Kalaea (Tongolele), the reptile woman. These secret rituals are dominated by a mysterious figure, "Damballah," who turns the victims into zombies. Determined to obtain the voodoo ringleader's identity, Capt. Labiche (Rafael Bertrand) and his police resort to interrogation and violence among the natives. In retaliation, Anabella (Ju-lissa), niece of Karl Van Molder (Boris Karloff) a large landowner, is kidnaped by the cult. She is chosen to be the next sacrificial victim.

Capt. Labiche and a fellow officer finally locate the secret ceremonial chamber in a deep cave. There, they discover the mysterious "Damballah" to be Van Molder. After they rescue Anabella, they demolish the chamber with dynamite. "Damballah" and the evil cult are finally destroyed forever.

NOTES

The Snake People was one of four films Karloff signed to make for Producer Luis Vergara. The Mexican filmmaker had obtained financing from Columbia Pictures to film them in Mexico. But due to the actor's emphysema problems in high altitudes, the Mexican actors and crew came to Hollywood and shot the four films back-to-back in the Hollywood Stage Studios in Los Angeles

With Rafael Bertrand.

instead. There, all of Karloff's scenes were filmed in five weeks during the spring of 1968.

Because of the featherbedding union problems, one American had to be hired for each of the Mexican crew. But the American crew did all of the production work while their Mexican counterparts did almost nothing.

During the filming, Karloff was physically in-capacitated by lung trouble, which necessitated an oxygen mask from time to time. Sensing that this might be their last opportunity, more and more Karloff fans visited the set armed with tape recorders, cameras and autograph books. After Karloff's scenes were completed, the crew returned to Mexico and shot the remaining scenes there.

As the mysterious Damballah.

With Yerye Beirute.

The Incredible Invasion

Columbia   1971.

CREDITS

Directed by Jack Hill *and* Juan Ibanez. *Screenplay by* Karl Schanzer *and* Luis Vergara. *Photography,* Austin McKinney *and* Raul Dominguez. *Color by* Eastman Color. Released April 1971. Running time: 90 minutes.

CAST

Boris Karloff, Enrique Guzman, Christa Linder, Maura Monti, Yerye Beirute, Tere Valez, Sergio Kleiner, Mariela Flores, Griselda Mejia, Rosangela Balbo and Tito Novarro.

SYNOPSIS

Prof. John Mayer (Boris Karloff) constructs a machine which will harness the destructive powers of a radioactive element. Impressed by its awesome powers, the military express interest in the machine as a potential weapon, but Mayer intends

With Enrique Guzman and
Christa Linder.

his machine to be used for the benefit of mankind. Fearful over the misuse of such a power, two aliens from outer space visit earth, intending to destroy Mayer's machine.

After they secretly enter the bodies of an escaped convict (Yerye Beirute) and Mayer, the convict murders Isabel (Maura Monti), a village girl. As the villagers storm Mayer's house, the convict attempts to murder the scientist's daughter, Laura (Christa Linder). But Mayer regains his will power and destroys the brute with his

machine. With the help of his assistant, Paul (Enrique Guzman), Mayer destroys the other alien. Aware that his invention would attract other aliens to earth, Mayer destroys his machine.

NOTES

The Incredible Invasion was the last feature film Karloff ever made. Owing to producer Vergara's death, his two remaining Karloff films (*The Fear Chamber* and *House of Evil*) have yet to be released.

With Viveca Lindfors and Jean-Pierre Aumont.

Cauldron of Blood

Cannon   1971.

CREDITS

Directed by Edward Mann. *Screenplay by* John Melson *and* Edward Mann. *Photography,* Francisco Sempere. *Color by* Eastman Color. Released August 1971. Running time: 101 minutes.

CAST

Jean–Pierre Aumont, Boris Karloff, Viveca Lindfors, Rosenda Monteros, Milo Queseda, Dianik Zurakowska and Ruben Rojo.

SYNOPSIS

Writer Claude Marchand (Jean–Pierre Aumont) visits the artist's colony in the Spanish village of Pinderera to do a story for a travel magazine. He obtains an interview with Franz Badulescu (Boris Karloff), the famous sculptor, and his wife, Tania (Viveca Lindfors). The sculptor has been blind since his wife attempted to murder him in order to inherit his fortune. Marchand also meets and falls in love with Valerie (Rosenda Monteros), a young painter. Soon, two people mysteriously disappear in the village, including Badulescu's model, Elga (Dianik Zurakowska).

Unknown to Badulescu, Tania and her lover, Shanghai (Milo Queseda), are plotting to kill him and are engaged in a series of gruesome murders. After secretly immersing the bodies in an acid bath, the skeletons are supplied as armatures to Badulescu who is involved in a complex work containing many figures. Valerie falls into the evil clutches of Tania and Shanghai who decide to make her the next victim for the sculptor's work.

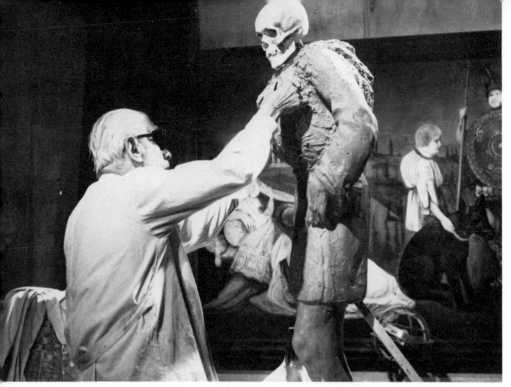

As Badulescu.

But Marchand arrives in time and rescues her. Learning of his wife's murderous plans and the origin of the other bodies, Badulescu kills Tania after a violent struggle. Half–mad with grief, the sculptor flings himself into the sea and drowns.

NOTES

Producer Robert D. Weinbach originally wanted Claude Rains for the role of Badulescu, but due to Rains's illness, he was replaced by Karloff. Originally titled *Blind Man's Bluff,* the film was shot in and around Madrid. Filming began in February 1967 and lasted almost three months.

REVIEW

. . . Since he's been dead nearly three years, Karloff's billing has been eliminated from some New York ads, a move which could hurt rather than help. It's the type of fare that audiences can take seriously or laugh at, being enjoyable either way. . . . Horror touches are well done even within the context of an obviously inexpensive production.

Box Office

With Rosenda Monteros and Viveca Lindfors.

BORIS KARLOFF on Television

Though Karloff's earliest appearances on television were through his Monogram features (1938–40) in 1948, he officially made his "live" debut the following year. Driven to keep practicing his craft constantly, Karloff also embraced the medium to escape motion picture type–casting.

In spite of the perishability of old kinescopes and erratic trade–paper listings of his early video appearances, the following chronology has been culled from over a thousand weeks of television programming. Brief bits and commercials have been disregarded. The dates are primarily New York City listings.

As Mother Muffin in *The Mother Muffin Affair* (Girl From U.N.C.L.E.).

With Mildred Natwick in
Starring Boris Karloff.

Karloff on Television

1949

CHEVROLET ON BROADWAY
NBC   Spring season.

Such stars as Jackie Cooper, Luise Rainer, Paul Muni, Jimmy Dunn, Eddie Albert, Janet Blair and Karloff made their TV debuts on this weekly live dramatic series.

CELEBRITY TIME
ABC   Sept. 4.

Panel—Conrad Nagel, host. Guest Karloff plugs his upcoming drama series.

STARRING BORIS KARLOFF
ABC   Sept. 22 – Dec. 15.

This thirteen-week dramatic series was aired on radio Wednesday nights by ABC, then televised on its (then) limited five–station TV network the following night. Titles of dramas: *Five Golden Guineas, The Mask, Mungahara, Mad Illusion, Perchance to Dream, The Devil Takes a Bride, The Moving Finger, The Twisted Path, False Face, Cranky Bill, Three O'Clock, The Shop at Sly Corner, Night Reveals.*

1950

MASTERPIECE PLAYHOUSE
NBC   Sept. 3.

Drama—*Uncle Vanya* by Chekov. Walter Abel, Eva Gabor, Karloff.

LIGHTS OUT
NBC   Sept. 18.

Drama—*The Leopard Lady.* Karloff in starring role.

PAUL WHITEMAN REVUE
ABC   Oct. 29.

Karloff in haunted house sketch for Halloween.

1951

DON McNEIL TV CLUB
ABC   Apr. 11.

Karloff guests in Chicago–based show.

TEXACO STAR THEATRE
NBC   Oct. 9.

Karloff joins Uncle Miltie.

With Peter Lorre in *All Star Revue*.

FRED WARING GE SHOW
    CBS   Oct. 21.

Karloff in Halloween production number.

ROBERT MONTGOMERY PRESENTS
    NBC   Nov. 19.

Drama—*The Kimballs* by Mitchell Wilson. Vanessa Brown, Richard Waring, Karloff.

CELEBRITY TIME
    CBS   Nov. 25.

Panel—Conrad Nagel, host. Kitty Carlisle, Karloff.

STUDIO ONE
    CBS   Dec. 3.

Drama—*Mutiny on the Nicolette* by Joseph Liss. Karloff as a mysterious stranger.

SUSPENSE
    CBS   Dec. 25.

Drama—*The Lonely Place*. Judith Evelyn, Robin Morgan, Karloff.

LUX VIDEO THEATRE
    CBS   Dec. 31.

Drama—*The Jest of Hahalaba* by Lord Dunsany. Karloff in starring role.

1952

COLUMBIA WORKSHOP
    CBS   Jan. 13.

Drama—*Don Quixote* by Cervantes. Karloff in starring role.

STORK CLUB
    CBS   Jan. 30.

Sherman Billingsley welcomes Karloff to the Cub Room.

TALES OF TOMORROW
    ABC   Feb. 22.

Drama—*Memento*. Karloff in starring role.

TEXACO STAR THEATRE
    NBC   Apr. 29.

Guests Don Cornell, Jimmy Nelson, Karloff joins Uncle Miltie.

CELEBRITY TIME
    CBS   May 25.

Panel—Conrad Nagel, host. Vivian Blaine, Orson Bean, Karloff.

CURTAIN CALL
    NBC   June 27.

Drama—*Soul of the Great Bell* by Lafcadio Hearn. Ballerina Raimonda Orselli, Karloff.

SCHLITZ PLAYHOUSE OF STARS
    CBS   July 4.

Drama—Irene Dunne, host. *Death House*. Toni Gerri, Karloff.

TEXACO STAR THEATRE
    NBC   Dec. 16.

Guests Don Ameche, Miriam Hopkins, Karloff join Uncle Miltie.

1953

HOLLYWOOD OPENING NIGHT
    NBC   Mar. 2

Drama—*The Invited Seven*. Karloff in starring role.

SUSPENSE
    CBS   Mar. 17.

Drama—*The Black Prophet*. Karloff as Rasputin.

ROBERT MONTGOMERY PRESENTS
    NBC   Mar. 30.

Drama—*Burden of Proof*. Karloff in starring role.

PLYMOUTH PLAYHOUSE
    ABC   May 24.

Drama—Sir Cedric Hardwicke, host. *The Chase* by John Collier. Philip Truex, Karloff. The latter also co-starred with Kyle McDonnell in *Reticence of Lady Anne* for this series, which also was called ABC ALBUM.

SUSPENSE
    CBS   June 23.

Drama—*The Signal Man* by Charles Dickens. Karloff in starring role.

RHEINGOLD THEATRE

Drama—*House of Death*. Karloff as Charles Branden.

1954

I'VE GOT A SECRET
    CBS   Oct. 13.

Panel—Garry Moore, host. Surprise guest Karloff has a secret for the panel.

CLIMAX!
    CBS   Dec. 16.

Drama—*White Carnation*. Karloff as Dr. Philip Nestri.

As the star of *Col. March of Scotland Yard*.

With Lee Grant, Christopher Plummer and Franchot Tone in *Even The Weariest River* (Alcoa Hour).

DOWN YOU GO
  Dumont   Dec. 17.

Panel—Dr. Bergen Evans, host. Karloff joins panel in word–game show.

COL. MARCH OF SCOTLAND YARD
  (Syndicated)   Dec.

Drama—Karloff in starring role of twenty-six half–hour shows produced by ITV Productions in England.

1955

BEST OF BROADWAY
  CBS   Jan. 5.

Drama—*Arsenic and Old Lace* by Joseph L. Kesselring. Helen Hayes, Billie Burke, Peter Lorre, Karloff as Jonathan Brewster.

DOWN YOU GO
  Dumont   Jan.

Panel—Dr. Bergen Evans, host. Karloff joins panel for month of January.

DONALD O'CONNOR
  NBC   Feb. 19.

Karloff sings two English music–hall tunes, "Human Thing to Do" and " 'Arry and 'Erbert."

ELGIN HOUR
  ABC   Feb. 22.

Drama—*The Sting of Death.* Karloff as Mr. Mycroft.

MAX LIEBMAN PRESENTS
  NBC   Mar. 12.

Musical—*A Connecticut Yankee* (*in King Arthur's Court*), based on 1927 Rodgers and Hart musical. Eddie Albert, Janet Blair, Karloff as King Arthur sings "Knight's Refrain" and "You Always Love the Same Girl."

WHO SAID THAT?
    Dumont   Apr. 30.

Panel—John K. M. McCaffery, host. Jimmy Cannon, Harriet Van Horne, Karloff.

GE THEATRE
    CBS   May 1.

Drama—*Mr. Blue Ocean*. Susan Strasberg, Eli Wallach, Anthony Perkins, Bramwell Fletcher, Karloff in title role.

I'VE GOT A SECRET
    CBS   Aug. 24.

Panel—Garry Moore, host.

U.S. STEEL HOUR
    CBS   Aug. 31.

Drama—*Counterfeit*. Karloff as George Redford.

1956

ALCOA HOUR
    NBC   Apr. 15.

Drama—*Even the Weariest River* by Alvin Sa-pinsley. Franchot Tone, Christopher Plummer, Karloff as Doc Dixon.

DUNNINGER
    NBC   July 18.

Karloff guests with the "mentalist."

FRANKIE LAINE
    CBS   Aug. 8.

ERNIE KOVACS
    NBC   Aug. 13.

CLIMAX!
    CBS   Sept. 6.

Drama—*Bury Me Later* by H. F. M. Prescott. Angela Lansbury, Torin Thatcher, Karloff as the Vicar.

PLAYHOUSE 90
    CBS   Oct. 25.

Drama—*Rendezvous in Black* by Cornell Woolrich. Franchot Tone, Laraine Day, Karloff as Ward Allen.

RED SKELTON
    CBS   Nov. 27.

Karloff joins Skelton in sketch.

With Julie Harris in *The Lark* (Hallmark Hall Of Fame).

277

$64,000 QUESTION
    CBS   Dec. 11, 18, 25.

Karloff chose category of children's stories, quit at $16,000 plateau.

1957

ROSEMARY CLOONEY
    NBC   Jan. 9.

Karloff as "Wolf–Grandmother" in Red Riding Hood sketch sings "You'd Be Surprised."

HALLMARK HALL OF FAME
    NBC   Feb. 10.

Drama—*The Lark* adapted by James Costigan. Julie Harris, Eli Wallach, Basil Rathbone, Karloff as Cauchon.

LUX VIDEO THEATRE
    NBC   Apr. 25.

Drama—*The Man Who Played God*, based on 1932 Arliss film and 1955 Liberace remake (*Sincerely Yours*). Karloff as Montgomery Royle.

KATE SMITH SPECIAL
    ABC   Apr. 28.

Guest Karloff sings "The September Song."

DINAH SHORE
    NBC   May 17.

Guest Karloff sings "Mama Look a' Boo Boo" and conducts an All–Ghoul Orchestra in sketch.

Singing on the *Dinah Shore Show*.

278

As Billy Bones in *Treasure Island* (Dupont Show Of The Month).

DINAH SHORE
    NBC   Oct. 27.

Karloff sings with Steiner Bros. and does Halloween sketch with kids.

ROSEMARY CLOONEY
    NBC   Oct. 31.

SUSPICION
    NBC   Dec. 9.

Drama—*The Deadly Game* by Friedrich Duerrenmatt. Gary Merrill, Joseph Wiseman, Karloff as Judge Winthrop Gelsey.

As the host of *Thriller*.

1958

BETTY WHITE SHOW
   ABC   Feb. 12.

Buster Keaton and Karloff in sketches.

TELEPHONE TIME
   ABC   Feb. 25.

Drama—*Vestris*. Karloff as Dr. Pierre.

SHIRLEY TEMPLE STORYBOOK
    NBC   Mar. 5.

Drama—*Legend of Sleepy Hollow*. Shirley Temple, John Ericson, Jules Munshin, Russell Collins, Karloff narrates.

STUDIO ONE
    CBS   Mar. 31.

Drama—*Shadow of a Genius* by Jerome Rise. Eva Le Gallienne, Skip Homeier, Karloff as nuclear scientist Prof. Theodore Koenig.

JACK PAAR
    NBC   Apr. 22.

Guests Charlie Weaver, Parker Fennelly, Elsa Maxwell, Karloff.

PLAYHOUSE 90
    CBS   Nov. 6.

Drama—*Heart of Darkness* by Joseph Conrad.

With Carolyn Kearney in *The Incredible Dr. Markesan* (Thriller).

With Tony Randall in *Arsenic and Old Lace* (Hallmark Hall Of Fame).

Roddy McDowell, Eartha Kitt, Oscar Homolka, Karloff as Kurtz.

THIS IS YOUR LIFE
NBC   Nov. 13.

Host Ralph Edwards surprises Karloff and recalls Boris' career in stage, film, radio and TV.

THE VEIL
(Pilot film for unsold series) Host.

1959

GALE STORM SHOW
CBS   Jan. 31.

It's Murder, My Dear. Gale Storm, Zasu Pitts, Karloff.

G. E. THEATRE
CBS   May 17.

Drama—*Indian Giver.* Edgar Buchanan, Carmen

With Marty Milner, Lon Chaney Jr., Peter Lorre and George Maharis in *Lizard's Leg and Owlet's Wing* (Route 66).

Mathews, Jackie Coogan, Karloff as Henry Church.

1960

PLAYHOUSE 90
     CBS   Feb. 9.

Drama—*To the Sound of Trumpets*. Judith Anderson, Stephen Boyd, Dolores Hart, Sam Jaffe, Karloff at Guibert.

DUPONT SHOW OF THE MONTH
     CBS   Mar. 5.

Drama—*Treasure Island*. Hugh Griffith, Max Adrian, Michael Gough, Karloff as Billy Bones.

HOLLYWOOD SINGS
     NBC   Apr. 3.

Tammy Grimes, Eddie Albert, Karloff hosts hour of song and sketches.

THRILLER
     NBC   Sept. 13.

Drama—Karloff hosted and occasionally acted in sixty-six one-hour shows. Premiere: *The Twisted Image*. George Grizzard.

THRILLER
     NBC   Nov. 22.

Drama—*The Prediction*. Audrey Dalton, Alex Davion, Karloff as Clayton Mace.

1961

THRILLER
  NBC   Oct. 2.

Drama—*The Premature Burial,* based on Edgar Allan Poe short story. Sidney Blackmer, Patricia Medina, Karloff as Dr. Thorne.

THRILLER
  NBC   Nov. 6.

Drama—*Last of the Sommervilles.* Phyllis Thaxter, Martita Hunt, Karloff as Dr. Farnham.

THRILLER
  NBC   Dec. 4.

Drama—*Dialogues with Death* (Two one-act dramas). (1) *Friend of the Dead.* Karloff as Pop Jenkins. (2) *Welcome Home.* Karloff as Col. Jackson.

1962

OUT OF THIS WORLD
  ABC

Karloff hosted a series of weekly (sixty-minute) science-fiction shows produced by BBC-TV in England.

HALLMARK HALL OF FAME
  NBC   Feb. 5.

Drama—*Arsenic and Old Lace* by Joseph L. Kesselring. Tony Randall, Dorothy Stickney, Mildred Natwick, Karloff as Jonathan Brewster.

PM   (Syndicated)   Feb. 12.

Mike Wallace, host. All-star tribute to George Schaefer. Tony Randall, Ed Wynn, Maurice Evans, Julie Harris, Kim Hunter, Karloff.

THRILLER
  NBC   Feb. 26.

Drama—*The Incredible Doktor Markesan.* Dick York, Carolyn Kearney, Karloff as Dr. Konrad Markesan.

THEATRE '62
  NBC   Mar. 11.

Drama—*The Paradine Case* by Robert Goldman, Richard Basehart, Viveca Lindfors, Robert Webber, Karloff as Sir Simon Flaquer.

ROUTE 66
  CBS   Oct. 26.

Drama—*Lizard's Leg and Owlet's Wing.* Lon Chaney Jr., Peter Lorre, Karloff played the Frankenstein Monster for the last time in this Halloween episode.

1963

HY GARDNER SHOW
  WOR   Mar. 3.

The Herald Tribune columnist interviews Peter Lorre and Karloff.

CHRONICLE
  CBS   Dec. 25.

Drama—*A Danish Fairy Tale.* The life of Hans Christian Andersen is told through four Andersen fairy tales. Karloff narrates.

1964

GARRY MOORE
  CBS   April 21.

Guests Alan King, Dorothy Loudon, Karloff.

1965

ENTERTAINERS
  CBS   Jan. 16.

Carol Burnett, Art Buchwald, Karloff, others.

SHINDIG
  ABC   Oct. 30.

Teen rock show with guests Jimmy O'Neill, Ted Cassidy, Karloff.

1966

WILD WILD WEST
  CBS   Sept. 23.

Drama—*Night of the Golden Cobra.* Robert Conrad, Ross Martin, Boris Karloff as Singh.

GIRL FROM U.N.C.L.E.
  NBC   Sept. 27.

Drama—*The Mother Muffin Affair.* Stefanie Powers, Robert Vaughn, Bruce Gordon, Karloff as Mother Muffin.

With Gene Barry in *The White Birch* (The Name Of The Game).

HOW THE GRINCH STOLE CHRISTMAS
    CBS   Dec. 18.

Animated cartoon of Dr. Seuss story. Animation director, Chuck Jones. Karloff narrates.

1967

I SPY
    NBC   Feb. 22.

Drama—*Mainly on the Plains*. Robert Culp, Bill Cosby, Karloff as Don Ernesto Silvando.

1968

RED SKELTON
    CBS   Sept. 24.

Karloff and Vincent Price in a mad–scientist sketch menace Clem Kadiddlehopper. Vincent and Boris sing "The Two of Us," kidding their horror films.

JONATHAN WINTERS SHOW
    CBS   Oct. 30.

Agnes Moorehead, Karloff as mad scientist in Halloween sketch. He also sings "It Was a Very Good Year."

THE NAME OF THE GAME
    NBC   Nov. 29.

Drama—*The White Birch*. Gene Barry, Ben Gazzara, Susan Saint James, Karloff as Orlov.

Afterword

Though Karloff is gone, they will argue that others will take his place as horror films continue to be made to satisfy the public demand. Some of this may be true, but in the early years of the Depression before the public was saturated by the pushbutton entertainment of television and the sex–and–gore color shockers masquerading as horror films, the public was anxious to forget their financial woes and flocked to the motion pictures because it was the cheapest form of entertainment available. In the darkened theatres, they watched in awe as Karloff's ghoulish creations came to life in *Frankenstein, The Mummy* and *The Ghoul,* unaware that the horror film was taking a definite form and shape, setting a pattern which would be repeated endlessly in the future. For a brief period, fear and anxiety filled their minds, making such petty matters as wondering where their next meal was coming from seem insignificant. Today, the younger generation obtains glimpses of Karloff's early films in the coziness of their homes on television, commercials permitting. It's not quite the same.

Despite this, the amount of pleasure Karloff and his contemporaries has given us will not be forgotten. His films will always find an audience because they fulfill a deep–rooted longing within us all—a love of the supernatural and the relentless curiosity of man to penetrate the unknown.